Daughter of
the Dales

Daughter of the Dales

The World of Hannah Hauxwell

Hannah Hauxwell
with Barry Cockcroft

CENTURY
London Sydney Auckland Johannesburg

also by Barry Cockroft
HANNAH IN YORKSHIRE
THE WAYS OF A YORKSHIRE DALE
THE DALE THAT DIED
PRINCES OF THE PLOUGH
A ROMANY SUMMER
A CELEBRATION OF YORKSHIRE
SEASONS OF MY LIFE

First published in 1990 by Random Century Group Ltd,
Random Century House, 20 Vauxhall Bridge Road,
London SW1V 2SA

Random Century Group Australia (Pty) Ltd,
20 Alfred Street, Milsons Point, Sydney,
New South Wales 2061, Australia

Random Century Group New Zealand Limited,
9–11 Rothwell Avenue, Albany, Auckland 10, New Zealand

Random Century Group South Africa (Pty) Ltd,
PO Box 337, Bergvlei, 2012 South Africa

Reprinted 1990 (six times)

British Library Cataloguing in Publication Data
Hauxwell, Hannah, *1926–*
Daughter of the Dales: the world of Hannah Hauxwell.
1. Yorkshire. Social life, 1901– – Biographies
I. Title II. Cockroft, Barry
942.81082092

ISBN 0–7126–4500–4

Colour photographs of Hannah Hauxwell by Mostafa Hammuri
Design by Behram Kapadia
Set in Linotronic Rockwell Light and Palatino
by Deltatype Ltd, Ellesmere Port

Printed and bound in Great Britain by
Butler & Tanner Ltd, Frome and London

Contents

Preface
The Leaving of Hannah

I don't know how I'll leave here . . . or how I'll feel after I have left. It will be a big upheaval, emotionally . . . physically . . . mentally . . .

It's just as though my world is falling to pieces. Everything I have known and been sure of . . . security, everything . . .

When Hannah Hauxwell made her reluctant exit from Baldersdale it was as if the elements conspired to invest it with special meaning. The entire valley shimmered with a glacial beauty as a four-wheel-drive-tractor, hazard light flashing, began to drag a hapless furniture van laden with her belongings out of its wild embrace.

Very few people saw snow that mild and benevolent winter but Baldersdale was not about to let its most cherished daughter go without a final salute.

It was a classic set piece encompassing all the glory – and the pain – of the place. The snow had fallen in unreasonable amounts and every corner was illuminated by that particular light which blesses the remoter regions where the air is unpolluted, casting an iridescent mantle which made the waters of Hunder Beck and the reservoir that feeds it dance like quicksilver. The same light silhouetted the farmhouse and the tall trees around it: Low Birk Hatt, home to the Hauxwells since it was built and the place where Hannah's spirit will always reside.

To me there's nowhere like it and never will be. This is my life – my world. And in years to come, if you see a funny old person – a ghost – walking up and down, it will be me.

And then came the concluding flourish.

As the convoy toiled upwards along the winding track, scattering sheep with icicled fleeces in its wake, a molten sunset began to spill slowly across the skyline.

Hannah left it all without a backward glance as though, in classic Homeric fashion, she knew she had to shut out the siren call. She sat in the cab of the van as if turned to stone, eyes glazed with tears.

She says she will never go back.

Wherever I am, whatever I am, a big part of me will be left here. Nowhere else . . .

That poignant moment in Hannah's life, that final severance of the chains which had bound her to Baldersdale far too long for her physical well-being, was essentially a private matter. Yet it was eventually shared by almost six and a half million people.

Tucked discreetly away behind a deep-frozen hillock, observing and recording the mournful event, was a camera crew, hardly believing their professional good fortune as nature turned on that slow-motion firework display.

For one man – the writer of this piece – there was a distinct sense of *déjà vu*. He had been there almost exactly seventeen years before, standing alongside a camera not very far from the same position, directing the very first film sequence ever shown of Hannah Bayles Tallentire Hauxwell.

Just like that afternoon, Baldersdale was deep in snow – indeed, a blizzard was blowing at the time.

And the scene was backlit by a stunning sunset.

And Hannah was towing a milk-white cow.

The first sequence . . . and now, almost two decades later, the last sequence. Two nearly identical situations. But so much had happened in between. Three major, internationally transmitted television documentaries, two best-selling books.

And the creation of a legend.

No one could have forecast the explosion of public interest created when Hannah emerged from that blizzard – and total obscurity – in the first Yorkshire Television programme, *Too*

Hannah with Barry Cockcroft during the making of Too Long a Winter *in 1972*

Long a Winter. That was remarkable enough but the way in which she moved with sublime serenity into a permanent position in the affections of a public which stretches far beyond the frontiers of this country was truly astonishing.

The most unlikely celebrity of them all transmits an aura which is almost royal in its nature. Everything she does or says automatically attracts the attention of an enormous audience. Every time she makes a public appearance the crowds turn out and queue for hours for a chance to get close to her. And some of

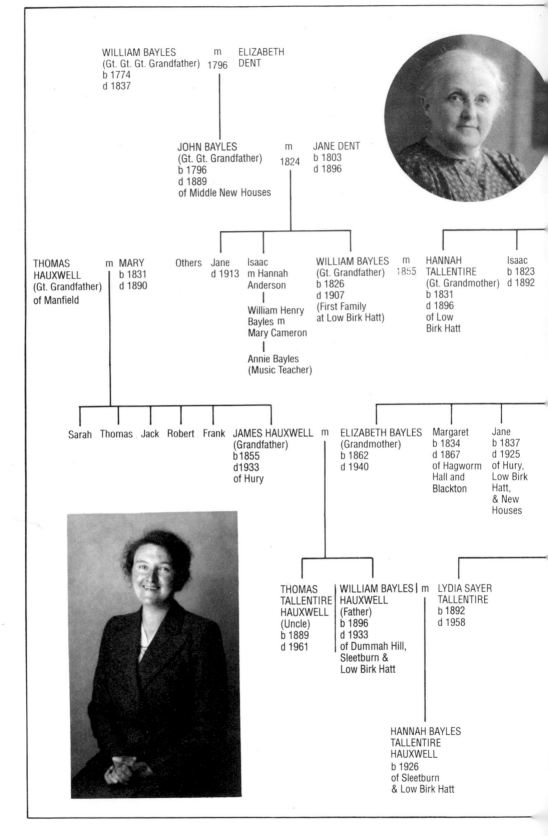

WILLIAM BAYLES   m   ELIZABETH
(Gt. Gt. Gt. Grandfather)   1796   DENT
b 1774
d 1837

JOHN BAYLES   m   JANE DENT
(Gt. Gt. Grandfather)   1824   b 1803
b 1796   d 1896
d 1889
of Middle New Houses

THOMAS   m   MARY   Others   Jane   Isaac   WILLIAM BAYLES   m   HANNAH   Isaac
HAUXWELL   b 1831   d 1913   m Hannah   (Gt. Grandfather)   1855   TALLENTIRE   b 1823
(Gt. Grandfather)   d 1890   Anderson   b 1826   (Gt. Grandmother)   d 1892
of Manfield   d 1907   b 1831
                                  William Henry   (First Family   d 1896
                                  Bayles m   at Low Birk Hatt)   of Low
                                  Mary Cameron   Birk Hatt

                                  Annie Bayles
                                   (Music Teacher)

Sarah   Thomas   Jack   Robert   Frank   JAMES HAUXWELL   m   ELIZABETH BAYLES   Margaret   Jane
                                     (Grandfather)   (Grandmother)   b 1834   b 1837
                                     b1855   b 1862   d 1867   d 1925
                                     d1933   d 1940   of Hagworm   of Hury,
                                     of Hury   Hall and   Low Birk
                                                                      Blackton   Hatt,
                                                                                & New
                                                                                Houses

THOMAS   WILLIAM BAYLES   m   LYDIA SAYER
TALLENTIRE   HAUXWELL   TALLENTIRE
HAUXWELL   (Father)   b 1892
(Uncle)   b 1896   d 1958
b 1889   d 1933
d 1961   of Dummah Hill,
                Sleetburn &
                Low Birk Hatt

HANNAH BAYLES
TALLENTIRE
HAUXWELL
b 1926
of Sleetburn
& Low Birk Hatt

HANNAH BAYLES TALLENTIRE HAUXWELL
FAMILY TREE

ISAAC TALLENTIRE (Gt. Gt. Grandfather) of Pike Stone, Holwick   m   ELIZABETH (BETTY) (Gt. Gt. Grandmother)

Margaret

Richard of Sleetburn & Low Fields S. Stainmore

Thomas b 1826 d 1903

WILLIAM TALLENTIRE (Gt. Grandfather)   m   LEE (Gt. Grandmother)

MARK SAYER (Gt. Grandfather)   m   — WALTON (Gt. Grandmother) of Manor House Farm, and Temperance Hotel, Bowes

Isaac b 1856 d 1935 of Dummah Hill

William b 1868 d 1934 of Low Birk Hatt

John
|
John Robert Norman Bayles (2nd cousin) m Lizzie Teasdale of Mickleton

James . John . Isaac b 1852 d 1915 of Grey Scar, Spittal

WILLIAM TALLENTIRE (Grandfather) of North Side, Bowes   m   ANNE SAYER (Grandmother)

James

Thomas b 1832 d 1909

Violet

Mary Anne

Maggie d 1919

Sarah d 1919

Isaac Thomas d 1919

Richard

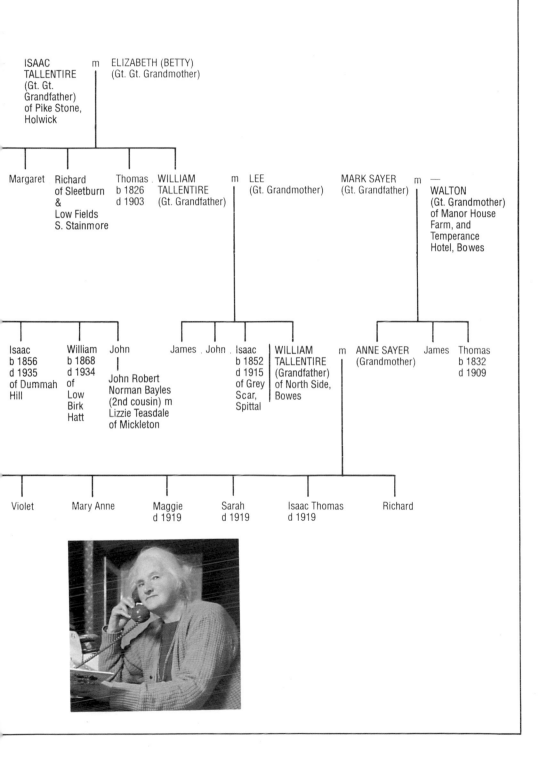

her admirers are almost too awestruck to speak when they are finally face to face with the lady.

If you try to analyse this phenomenon coldly and clinically, it all seems a total aberration. For instance, the third and final documentary, *A Winter Too Many*, had a storyline which would have been laughed to scorn under normal circumstances. A full hour of network time devoted to some elderly lady in a half-abandoned dale trying to decide whether or not to leave her farm and go into a retirement cottage?

Totally ridiculous!

But that programme was hailed as the most popular of the year. Over 6 million people watched – more than double the average for a late-night documentary – and, judging from the response it drew, a fair proportion could scarcely see for tears. The mail certainly flooded in, all exceedingly appreciative and most demanding a repeat. Even before that success, Hannah was firmly fixed in the celebrity rota of the Press, which monitors her progress constantly and sends its best writers to pen a stream of in-depth interviews (and even the most hardboiled and cynical of them melt in the warmth of her simple honesty).

Hannah's journey from the deprivation of the years alone and unknown, working a merciless hill farm, living on the pitiful sum of £280 a year (and paying for animal-feed out of that), with no basic amenities such as electricity or water on tap, via an unprecedented tidal wave of public adulation, to that heart-rending farewell to the place she holds so dear, has been a self-perpetuating saga unique in the annals of modern folklore.

And now the story of Hannah Hauxwell moves into another phase: the next chapter of a life which has fascinated thousands of people from all sectors of the social spectrum, who see in this lady a quality so fundamental and inspirational that it transcends all barriers and casts a spell which cannot conclusively be explained.

1

Hannah's New Life: Coping with Civilization – and The Great One

It was clear that Hannah would not consider moving far from her native heath and, after lengthy deliberations, settled on a cottage in Cotherstone which stands five miles away from Low Birk Hatt at one of the entrances to Baldersdale. It's a well-founded Dales village, mentioned in the Domesday Book, with a fascinating and somewhat turbulent, if bizarre, history. Cotherstone Castle, which loomed over the confluence of the rivers Tees and Balder, is now just a heap of rubble. But it certainly saw some action. Last occupied in 1315, it was the ancestral home of the Fitzhughs but passed by marriage out of the family when the last of the male line died in a hunting accident while pursuing his quarry clean over a cliff, if local legend is correct. Then the Scots raided down from the borders and put it to the torch. A lot of the stone went to build houses for the local peasants, who apparently had a tough time. They were once so poverty-stricken they were known through the valley of the Tees as people who 'christened calves, hoppled lops and knee-banded spiders'. That meant they could afford so few cattle that each one had a name (a tradition perpetuated by Hannah!), and lops (lice) and spiders had their legs tied together to prevent them running away.

The area suffered badly during the time of the plague, which gave rise to the legend of the Butterstone. It stands in splendid isolation near the moorland road to Bowes and it was there that merchants and farmers would leave butter, eggs and other foodstuffs to be picked up by the afflicted. They were obliged to leave their money in a bowl of vinegar to – it was hoped – ward off contamination.

Life proceeds at a gentle, traditional pace today for the 500 or so residents of Cotherstone. Kelvin Walker runs his general store and petrol pumps (and taxi service), the Post Office also sells the superb Cotherstone cheese, and there are two excellent public houses.

Belle Vue Cottage is very conveniently situated for all these amenities, and a distinct *frisson* of excitement ran through the community when it became known that Hannah Hauxwell was the new owner.

Now, it's a funny thing, but in the days when there was a weekly bus service out of Baldersdale it went past Belle Vue cottage on the way to Barnard Castle and I used to look at it and say to myself, 'Well, that's an ugly place, I wouldn't like to live there!'

I don't wish to be disrespectful, and everybody has a right to their own taste, but it was the colour of it that really put me off. It was painted in a kind of orange. Someone obviously agreed with me eventually and it was changed to its present cream colour, which is a vast improvement.

Oddly enough, I had been interested in it three or four years ago when it was on the market prior to being bought by the lady who sold it to me. I was being taken somewhere by car and a stop had been made at Kelvin's petrol pumps opposite. There was a 'For Sale' sign outside, and at the time I was beginning to contemplate leaving Baldersdale – half of me wanted a more suitable place and the other half was telling me to stop at Low Birk Hatt. So I had a look at it from the outside and I changed my original opinion. It seemed to have a good deal going for it.

But the one thing that you cannot change, unlike the colour, is the fact that it faces north. Most of the living accommodation at Low Birk Hatt faces north and I always thought that when I moved I would definitely have a south-facing house. I didn't fancy north again at all. But there is a saying, is there not: 'Man proposes, and God disposes!'

What it does have – and this is a very important thing for me, having lived for so many years in an isolated place – is a certain amount of privacy. When one has been used to the nearest neighbours being several fields away, it wouldn't do to have someone else's door or window overlooking every part of the house. The whole of one side of Belle Vue Cottage is quite private, and I count that a real blessing.

The other factor that appealed to me was the size of the

rooms. They are very nicely proportioned for a cottage. The lounge has a large bay window with a beautiful view of the village and I can sit there and watch the world go by, if I feel like it.

And then I have always fancied a little hall and stairs because at the farm the stairs came straight down to the front door. Now I have stairs which actually turn the corner into a splendid hall. You get less draughts that way.

There are two good-sized bedrooms and a box-room but the real luxury is the bathroom. I never had such a thing before, and I am like a child when it comes to running water. Mind, I can always claim to have had running water at Low Birk Hatt but it did happen to be a stream some way down the meadow. When you've been used to that for sixty-two years, hot water and a flushing toilet do come as something of a culture shock.

Then there is the telephone. Until I arrived here I tended to regard the telephone with some trepidation. It took a good deal of time for me and it to get together. I used to wonder what on earth people found to talk about for so long, and on the occasion when I was called to a neighbour's telephone in Baldersdale, I was so uneasy that someone had to hold it to my ear. But that has all changed now. I find it a very useful thing, and I am as bad as the next person at chatting merrily away with little thought of time or the expense of it. If there is one drawback to life at Belle Vue Cottage, it is the lack of land around the place. There is a small strip of garden at the front but nothing at the back or side, not even a yard. I have to rely on the kindness of a good neighbour to hang out my washing. But I came to terms with all that because the house has so much going for it in other ways.

Small it may be, but that postage stamp of a garden at the front of the house does boast a distinction which falls to but a few: two rose bushes of a rather particular, not to say exclusive, variety.

I must admit that my first few days in my new home were quite strange and a little frightening. I kept hearing these small explosions and I wondered what could possibly be the

A view of old Cotherston (sic) (Courtesy of Darlington Library)

cause. Then I cottoned on that it was the gas central-heating boiler coming on. It's such a wonderful thing and gives out such heat that I spend quite a lot of my time sitting alongside it in the kitchen. It seems to have a mind of its own, and I call it The Great One.

Mrs Pearson, the nice old lady who sold Belle Vue Cottage to me, set the controls a few days before she left and said the milkman understood how it worked and he would help me if I had need of it. Now I am not at one with technology such as electricity and things like that. Unless it is an easy switch-on or switch-off I tend to be lost. I am more geared to old things, and

Hannah's cottage – a summer view

The Great One does play some funny tricks sometimes. It once went cold, although the little red lights were still on. I didn't bother the milkman, but a lady kindly came and put in a little battery – and then the neighbours adjusted it and got it going. I still haven't a clue how it works.

I also have an automatic washing machine but it has to be by the sink for the water to be pumped out and it has no wheels. So I still wash by hand with my blue-bag and my plunger. There's a little spin-dryer too, but I haven't got around to using that either.

Now Mrs Pearson was most kind to me over the sale of the house – indeed, but for her kindness I would probably never have got it. Several people were after it, but when she knew I wanted it she sent a message saying she preferred me to have it. I think maybe she had seen the television programmes and was favourably disposed.

I finally moved in just before Christmas 1988 and, like Edith Piaf, I have no regrets. Everyone in the village is most friendly.

One problem is the constant flow of visitors who arrive unannounced on my doorstep. They are all very welcome, of course, although they park their cars in inconvenient places, but they do not help in the problems I have in finding the time to sort out my new home. Most of my stuff is still in packing-cases and, because I am not a very quick person, it is likely I will remain in a disorganized state for some time to come. Of course, I have this terrible failing: I am a hoarder. I cannot bear to throw things away, partly because of my upbringing and partly out of sentiment.

I suppose I have enough to fill two cottages, so space is at a premium before I have even unpacked half of what I brought. One very generous gentleman in London, who imports pianos from Poland and who heard me playing the organ in the programmes, has offered me a brand-new piano as a gift. I would like to have it very much because music is one of the great pleasures in life to me but I just have nowhere to put it at the moment.

There are so many demands on my time. Quite apart from my visitors and my new friends, some of whom whisk me away to stay for the weekend, there are what you could call my 'professional engagements'. By that I mean book-signing sessions – I've been all over the place, from Darlington and Beverley in the North, to as far as Nottingham in the South, and met some wonderful people – and literary luncheons, plus what I suppose you could call 'personal appearances' at all kinds of functions.

So it is very difficult to achieve what one might call a set pattern in life. Back at Low Birk Hatt there was no such problem because the demands of the seasons, and particularly the daily needs of my animals – my family, as you could call them – filled every waking moment.

On the days when I am left to my own devices I am a bit of a disgrace really. I get up at a rather late hour. Indeed I have my breakfast at dinner-time, somewhere around 11.30 a.m. – that's the time for the main meal of the day in farming circles since it is normal for those who live from the land to rise at first light. Now, I was never a good getter-up but I do have the excuse that I often retire very late, particularly if I have a visitor in the afternoon and need to get a bit of washing or something done at night when it is possible to get on with it without interruptions. All in all, I suppose I have changed to something of a nightbird. There is a good social life in the village, and I wish I had a chance to become more involved. I have been to the Over-Sixties Club where they have some very good concerts and I go to services at Cotherstone Methodist Chapel whenever I can.

There is no routine. I suppose routines and me don't go together.

2

Health, Wealth...
and the Perils of
Civilization

Hannah Hauxwell's somewhat late introduction to the benefits of modern civilization, such as water that arrived at the turn of a tap, central heating, shops just a few yards away, even a telephone (the number is ex-directory or it would never stop), clearly created a revolution in her life. Her financial situation also improved dramatically, with a tidy amount left from the sale of Low Birk Hatt to invest, and substantial sums from the royalties of her best-selling book. But what no one could foresee were the complex problems of readjustment. For instance, the emotional strain of leaving Baldersdale almost certainly reduced her resistance to the germs and viruses that also come with the overall package of civilization. Less than a year after her arrival in Cotherstone, a crisis occurred.

It started on a Friday night in November when I felt a bit odd, so I took a Paracetamol and went to bed with a hot-water bottle. Next day I didn't feel so bad and I made an appearance for a charity – I really had to do it – then went to visit a relative the following day. But by the Tuesday night my throat had all dried up and, though I tried to motor on, I had to take to my bed on the Wednesday. I thought it would only take a couple of days to clear up, but it was to take quite a lot longer.

I'm afraid that when I dropped out of sight it created a great deal of concern in the village. A friend who had a key let herself in and called upstairs, but I didn't want anyone to come into the bedroom because they might catch whatever it was I had. And I didn't want to bother with a doctor – in Baldersdale you were used to dealing with minor complaints on your own. But as time dragged on and I obviously got worse, I suppose my friends decided to take action. A doctor was called out and he diagnosed some kind of virus and prescribed a course of antibiotics.

That should have been the end of it but it most certainly was not. Altogether it lasted a month and but for the neighbours rallying around and taking care of me I would have ended up in hospital.

For day after day I couldn't even keep water down. Everything tasted horrible. But Elsie Birdsall and Lavinia Thwaites kept coming in with all kinds of things to try and get me going – home-made soups, arrowroot, custards – and finally I began to mend a little.

I know one or two people had begun to despair of me ever getting better at one point but, basically, I have been blessed with a strong constitution. There are one or two worries, such as the blood pressure and a touch of angina. And I suppose it might have been serious had I been at Low Birk Hatt on my own with no help when that virus struck me down. But then, the air is purer and germs less prevalent there.

I did get the usual childhood ailments, though, such as mumps, measles and chicken-pox. So Baldersdale wasn't that free of infection. Mind, I welcomed them with open arms because it meant I could stay off school. But one summer when I was around ten or eleven I developed a nasty sore throat which the doctor thought was tonsillitis. Then I started to be sick and my skin started to peel and drop off. You see, it turned out to be scarlet fever, which is a notifiable disease. But by the time everyone, including the doctor, realized what it was it was just too late. Mother had told Mrs Archer at Baldersdale school that it was tonsillitis and I'm not sure that she ever did find out the reality of it. As far as I know, no one else in the Dale caught it – except my Uncle Tommy, my father's brother who had come to run the farm for us when my father died at such a tragically early age. I think we must have both picked it up during a visit to some relatives in Piercebridge.

It was Mother who nursed us through it and it was an experience I wouldn't like to repeat. It took about six weeks for the fever to go and then we got sulphur candles to fumigate the house from top to bottom. I suppose if the doctor had got his diagnosis right, then I would have had to go to hospital but it was to be another ten years before I was sent to such a place.

A rare picture of Hannah, recently unearthed, taken shortly after her mother's death in 1958

I had been poorly for a while and couldn't eat and the doctor thought it may be appendicitis so he sent me to Darlington Hospital. I was scared at the prospect of an operation but, thankfully, it didn't prove necessary. I didn't like hospital at all that time because such strange things happened in the night with nurses coming and going and moving people and giving injections. In fact, in the middle of one night they came and moved my bed to another part of the hospital without saying a word to me.

The next time I needed serious medical attention was quite a different experience. I had just had my forty-first birthday and had been going through a very unhappy time, not eating properly because I was economizing so much, and becoming properly run down. Of course, by then I was completely on my own and the doctor told me that I must go into hospital – this time at Northallerton.

They were ever so grand there. I went in feeling very poorly and not much good for anything and came out a new woman. Mind, it took about eight weeks to achieve that desirable state, and all they did was to give me some tablets, good food, rest and lots of kindness. I should have been discharged earlier but I had developed a cold and they insisted I stay until it had completely cleared up.

I met some wonderful people in that place. There was one lady with a very posh voice, a doctor's widow, who had been in Jarrow at the time of that terrible hunger march. She was a big woman and had suffered a stroke. I noticed that she looked a bit unhappy so I went across to her, worried that she might be a bit of a madam and wouldn't like to associate with the likes of me. But we became the firmest of friends and kept in touch by letter afterwards until she sadly died. There were several others who used to come and see me in Baldersdale, particularly after the first television programme went out in January 1973, including some of the nurses. They were so marvellous those nurses, some of them so young and all so dedicated. I think nurses are born, not made. Speaking of television, I had my first taste of the magic box in that hospital. They allowed us to watch it in the dayroom until 10.00 p.m. But, to be honest, I wasn't that keen. I have to admit I was sorry to leave Northallerton Hospital. It was lonely when I came back to Low Birk Hatt.

Now, as far as my health is concerned these days it could be a little bit better but a bonny sight worse. I take pills every day for my blood pressure, and I have some others, little things, ready for when I get what I call chuntering pains in my chest. And there's a bit of rheumatism in my right shoulder and arm which is something of a nuisance. When I was convalescing after that last virus, my Good Samaritans in Cotherstone arranged for me to have the Meals on Wheels service for several weeks. They were excellent and built up my strength nicely.

Even before that I had put on some weight which didn't all drain away during my illness. I don't know what I weigh now, but I can tell from the mirror and the clothes that I wear that there is, sadly, more of me than there was.

It could be about twelve years ago since I last weighed myself. There weren't many weighing machines in Baldersdale, but then a friend had to get one because of health problems and I turned out to be something around ten stones. Goodness knows what it is now.

I have friends who worry that I don't eat well and regularly enough but I suppose it is all a continuation of the habits formed when I was a one-woman farmer. I always like butter and toast for my breakfast – never bacon because that is a dinner dish. Sometimes dinner comes and sometimes it does not. It all depends on the time I can find to prepare it. During the hot summers I've had a lot of lettuce and tomato with maybe a bit of fruit. Last summer I really lived it up because I treated myself to some peaches.

And now I find myself eating tomatoes in the winter, which must be considered something of a luxury.

But it seems that I cannot rid myself of this fear of running short of money. It is in the system and has been for as long as I can recall. I know that I have a comfortable income now, but I still have difficulty in believing it. The brake is still on financially. I tend to live on my pension and, even when I see something I need, I will try and think of a reason to manage without.

For instance, in Kelvin Walker's shop across the road there are some brushes that I need. I'll ask him all about them and look at them but I keep putting off buying them. I know it seems like madness, but it's something I just cannot help.

The artist Trevor Stubley at work on a portrait of Hannah which was exhibited at the National Portrait Gallery

If you ask me how I would indulge myself if forced to, I suppose I would put some comfortable footwear near the top of the list. Then perhaps some joints of meat, or a fowl. I cannot do it yet but I am trying to come round to it. One is constantly reminded that life is short, so I suppose I should. But then I don't do too badly, and people mustn't worry so much about me.

3

Hannah's Secrets… and the Return of Rosa, the Senior Cow

Like all maiden ladies, Hannah Hauxwell has her secrets. And she can spring a surprise. Not long after acquiring Belle Vue Cottage she began to search for a piece of land in the Cotherstone area, preferably a fenced-in meadow. It soon became a matter of urgency. Puzzled friends were informed, as they set about helping her to find something, that it was necessary to afford Hannah some privacy – somewhere the daily stream of visitors wouldn't know about, somewhere she could escape to and sit and dream in solitude. But it transpired eventually that wasn't the only reason. Those who saw her last television programme, *A Winter Too Many*, will remember the extremely poignant sequence – and the tears – when she said farewell to her 'family', the beloved beasts, as they wended their way down the road from Low Birk Hatt to new ownership, led by the senior cow – 'Rosa, my lovely Rosa' – who had given Hannah the only available warm drink, her milk, and acted as a radiator when the power failed at Low Birk Hatt during the last savage winter. Well, it turned out that Rosa wasn't sold at all. She still belongs to Hannah, and is merely boarding out. Eventually, some land was found, and the lady who finds it psychologically impossible for the moment to afford a piece of meat parted with a substantial sum without demur.

I hope people will understand when I say I don't want to reveal exactly where it is. The need to have my own quiet corner became a priority during my first Easter in Cotherstone, when I was a bit depressed. I was suffering from a cold, the first for years – in fact I cannot recall the last time I had a cold – and because the weather was nice the village was extremely busy with tourists and lots of traffic and people knocking on my door. I thought to myself that I had landed up in a place without an inch of ground to call my own.

Now please understand that I really do like my visitors.

They are, with few exceptions, very kind and generous and come from far and near, even from overseas. Some have become true friends, and I have spent several weekends away because of their thoughtfulness. One couple who own an apartment in the south of Spain are even trying to persuade me to go there. But to travel to foreign parts is something I have never done and can scarcely contemplate. But the time might come!

They keep on calling me a celebrity, but I cannot really accept that. I am just an ordinary Daleswoman and if I began to think or act otherwise I know a few people around here who would soon bring me to my senses. But I have to concede that an amazing number of people are interested in me because of the television programmes and the books. Everyone needs a bit of time to themselves so something had to be done.

I was very lucky to find this piece of land. It's only about a quarter of an acre, but it's quite idyllic, and within reasonable reach of home. And I might be able to bring down Rosa for a bit during the summertime so we can renew our friendship. But I'm not sure whether it can be a permanent home for her because the fencing might not be good enough if she becomes lonely and tries to get out. Most animals like company, you know.

Quite apart from Rosa, it is necessary for me to have somewhere to go and think without interruption. Even if the weather is bad I'll still be able to slip away there because it has a shelter which was included in the sale.

I do miss Rosa, and I am not able to go and see her because she is being looked after by my friend, Bill Purves at Clove Lodge, the next farm to Low Birk Hatt. I am afraid I cannot bear just yet to go back to Baldersdale. Nor have I been able to watch *A Winter Too Many*.

I have thought about going up to Clove Lodge in the dark to say hello to Rosa, when I wouldn't be able to see my old place. You have to understand that no one but my family had ever lived at Low Birk Hatt before I sold it. My great-grandfather, William Bayles, was the first to occupy it and he was born in 1826. To go back and see it now might just upset the balance of

things at a crucial time, when I am trying to make a very difficult adjustment to my life.

I still have a foothold in Baldersdale, which is not widely known. Further down the valley from Low Birk Hatt is a place I own called Walker Hall, which has 17 acres of land. I was just not prepared to let that go when I sold Low Birk Hatt because it was my parents' dream house. They were going to retire there.

You see, they never really had a place of their own. They always had to share with other people, our elderly relatives. Walker Hall was bought long ago by Daddy's mother, Grandma Hauxwell, when she and Grandad were living at Hury in a place called Yew Tree. They never actually moved in and they promised it to Daddy.

Walker Hall may well be one of the oldest houses in Baldersdale. I believe it had a thatched roof and it was such a bonny place, but it has sadly been derelict for years. The last family to live there was called Wright, but that was well before my time.

It faces south, and had a little garden with trees all around. The thatched roof went long ago, but when I was a child the loft was still covered and Mother and Father kept a bed there and a few other necessary things. The three of us used to go down in summer to stay and do the haymaking. It's a lovely memory. Mother would cook on an open fire, the birds sang in the trees, and there was a bush in the corner which had white blossom, and roses grew wild everywhere. We all slept in the same bed, and it was so cosy.

I liked the design of the place very much. It had a nice square kitchen with one long window and a little narrow one, both with stone lintels. The kitchen opened into a very pleasant sitting-room, which had a door leading to a little dairy on the right and then to the stairs which had a half-landing with a tiny window looking out at the back. I think the

A discreet view of Hannah's hiding place – the small field where she hopes Rosa the cow may come to visit

Haytime in Baldersdale – the Hind family of Clove Lodge, once Hannah's neighbours. Probably taken between the wars.

stairs were constructed of stone but it's hard to tell because it's been deep in rubble ever since I can recall. There were two good bedrooms, both with fireplaces, and I believe another small one over the dairy. The door of the back kitchen went down two steps and then there was a chimney corner with shaped stonework, which I think would have had a wooden seat long ago.

Although there was – still is – a tree growing through the middle of the house, the stone walls had been well built and still stand to this day. Daddy was going to rebuild it with his own hands and had already done a bit to it when I was young. He put in a little stone trough to catch the water from a stream at the back, and bought a fireplace with an iron range oven and grate, especially for Walker Hall. He and Mother must have thought a great deal of the place to go to that expense at a time when money was so short.

Daddy had so many plans for Walker Hall but then he had so little time to do much. He died of pneumonia about twelve years after he bought Low Birk Hatt.

He was only thirty-seven.

4

Hard Life and the Hauxwells: the Untold Story of Hannah's Mother and Father

'The Hard Life' – that was the television series title of *Too Long a Winter*. People were totally amazed that, in Britain in the second half of the twentieth century, someone could be living in such materially deprived conditions, alone, with no water on tap and no electricity, on an income of barely £5 a week – and that she could rise above it with such dignity, inner tranquillity and gentle philosophy.

And yet, the burden of life that her mother and father, separately and together, had to bear far exceeds that which Hannah endured, and may explain in some measure the genesis of Hannah's fortitude and sublime character, which have inspired so many.

Hannah may have gone without most of the comforts that people take for granted, but at least she had emotional warmth and stability, wrapped as she was in the cocoon of a caring family – her mother, grandparents, and for a little time her tragic father, all around her.

Not so her mother and father. Their lives were far more than just hard. And there were strange parallels in the patterns of their childhood. Hannah has never told their story before . . .

Father was a Baldersdale man, born and bred, brought up at Hury, lower down the Dale. Grandfather James Hauxwell met Grandmother Elizabeth, who was a Bayles, when he came to work on the building of the reservoir, just below Low Birk Hatt. He had been in the Army, had served in India, and knew a bit about the world. Although I loved him dearly, he was a bit of a rascal and liked the drink far too much. They took Yew Tree Farm at Hury, next to Walker Hall, and then moved to Nelson House. They had two sons, my father and Uncle Tommy, and I think another child who didn't survive.

Now, there was a bachelor brother of Grandmother's, my Great-Uncle Isaac, who had a farm called Dummah Hill at

North Stainmore. I imagine the family considered that my father would be better off living with him because of the atmosphere created by my grandfather's drinking. Daddy must have been quite young when he left, because he went to school at North Stainmore.

Oddly enough, a similar thing happened to my mother. Her mother, my Grandmother Anne, was a Sayers, and they were the Manor House family in Bowes and rather better off than most. They may even have had servants, and I remember seeing photographs of her in a beautiful gown. Sadly, I only ever saw my grandmother a couple of times so I never came to know her. She married into the Tallentire family, who owned the pub called New Spittal in the same area but relinquished the licence because of their Methodist beliefs. But the Tallentires were farmers and used to the physical hardships that go hand-in-hand with life on the land. Not that they didn't have an appreciation of the arts because they were a very musical family. And it was generally accepted that Grandad William Tallentire was capable of making his way in any society, so it really wasn't a clear case of Grandma marrying beneath her. The pub they used to have was patronized by shooting parties in the grouse season and one big businessman was so impressed by Grandad that he offered to take him back with him to train him for a position in his firm. But nothing came of it in the end.

Becoming a farmer's wife must have been very difficult for Grandma. She was rather young when she married and had been brought up as a lady, so it was another world for her. I can really sympathize with the situation in which she found herself. Then the children started coming along – rather quickly, I fear, and seven in number, which didn't help matters one bit. Her health began to suffer, which was understandable, and I think at one time she deteriorated so badly that the doctors rather washed their hands of her. But Grandad Tallentire persevered and nursed her through. So when Grandad's uncle, Richard Tallentire, asked if they could bring Mother up, they agreed to let her go. I believe she was very young – just a little thing – but it must have seemed the

North Stainmore School. Hannah's father in Eton collar, back row, behind the long-haired girl in white dress.

best thing to do in the circumstances. You see, Richard and his wife, Elizabeth, known as Aunt Bessie, had lost the only child they ever had. He was a little boy called Thomas Isaac, who must have been very dear to his poor parents. Mother said that Aunt Bessie was fond of telling one story about Thomas Isaac, recalling the occasion when he was asked to say grace before breakfast one morning and steadfastly refused although commanded several times by his father. When asked several times for an explanation he eventually said very plaintively, 'Daddy, you don't say grace for porridge!' It was considered by the family to be a very amusing incident.

He was only about four when he died and I think it was totally unexpected, because I believe that the doctor who had tended him had remarked previously that he wished his own son, who was about the same age as Thomas Isaac, had been as robust. His death was not due to any lack of care because they owned their own house and were reasonably well off. It was just one of those tragic quirks of fate.

His father was very proud of his house because he had built it on a bit of land at Low Fields and did quite a lot of the construction work himself, with the help of his bachelor brother, Tommy. I know that when it was finished, he turned to his wife and announced triumphantly: 'There, Bessie. Now you can bide in your own house.' That was another oft-told story in our family because it must have meant a lot in those days, owning your own house instead of paying rent to a landlord.

So Mother filled the gap in their lives. It was a good home but both Richard, who was a bearded gentleman, and Bessie were rather strict. Mother told me that once when she had gone with them to chapel – and she was only a tot – she had just a little peep around at the rest of the congregation. Immediately a hand was placed firmly over her head and turned it to face the front again. The hand, of course, belonged to her great-uncle and foster father. Unfortunately, he did not live very long. His brother, Tommy, came to live in the house but he didn't survive very long either. There was so much sadness, so many funerals in my mother's childhood. Anyway, Aunt Bessie brought her up in the little house built by her husband and brother-in-law which was near to South Stainmore. And, just over the hill at North Stainmore, at Dummah Hill, Great-Uncle Isaac Bayles was looking after Daddy, and training him to be a farmer.

There is no doubt that both had hard lives. Mother served her time as a dressmaker with a maiden lady who had a business in Kirkby Stephen and made a bit of money that way. But she also had to keep house for Aunt Bessie and for a lodger she had to take in to make ends meet. He was a schoolteacher and a very nice man, I understand, but there wasn't much opportunity for Mother to go out and have a little enjoyment and apparently Aunt Bessie did not encourage such things. She had a sister who was much more understanding. Mother called her Aunt Mary, and thought she was a grand woman. She had children of her own, you see, and would try and persuade Aunt Bessie to be a little less strict with Mother. 'Let her be', she would say. 'Let her have a bit of enjoyment.'

Then Aunt Bessie had a stroke, more than one in fact, and burned herself rather badly, because she apparently suffered one when she was bending down to tend the fire. That meant Mother had to quit her dressmaking career since Aunt Bessie couldn't be left alone afterwards. Of course, that created an extra burden. I don't know how she managed to find the time, but when she got older she also played the organ for the Sunday services at the local Methodist chapel, as well as running the choir practices.

It may have been at the chapel that Father began to court Mother. She never really said. But they would have met when both the Tallentire brothers became ill and died and something had to be done about the farming land that went with Aunt Bessie's house at Low Fields. Great-Uncle Isaac at Dummah Hill, where Father was living and working, was kin to the brothers so an arrangement was made for him to take over the land. Of course, that meant extra work for everyone at Dummah Hill, particularly Father. It wasn't an easy courtship because there was so little time to spare after the day's labour was over. In fact, with Daddy it was all work –

apparently he put in some ridiculous hours. He was so conscientious, and the conditions were not good. Uncle Tommy, his only brother, used to tell me, in jocular fashion, that the only difference between Daddy and himself was that Daddy went into work and he ran away from it. Grandmother used to say that if it had been possible to take their personalities and shake them together a bit it would have been better for both of them.

I still have some letters which Mother and Father wrote to each other – beautiful letters, which are a revelation of their lives, both when they were courting and after they were married. Mother, who was two or three years older, used to worry herself sick about the way he toiled, going on every hour sent in all weathers, and not stopping to change into dry

opposite, *Hannah's mother as a young woman*

below, *Hannah's father as a young man*

clothes when the weather was wet. They could only snatch a few minutes together from time to time, usually when Daddy came over to Low Fields to look after the cattle, or during the haytiming.

In time, they decided to get married and Mother made her own wedding dress from a roll of silk given to her by her mother. I still have it. The wedding was held in 1920 at Mouthlock Methodist Chapel, at South Stainmore, where Mother was the organist and, much to her surprise and delight, the members of the chapel presented them with an inscribed silver teapot. It became a great treasure because there wasn't much money to spare in those days. But it was solid silver – and the inscription must have cost a bit as well. I keep it safely tucked away.

It was a nice wedding, necessarily modest. Uncle Tommy was Daddy's best man and Mother's sister, Violet, was the bridesmaid. Grandad Tallentire gave away the bride and I think Grandad Hauxwell performed one of his well-known recitations. I do believe they wore top hats, but there are none of the usual wedding photographs to confirm that. Daddy thought that photography would be too expensive and Mother declared that she wasn't bothered. I can't imagine how, given their circumstances, but they did manage to afford a week's honeymoon by the sea in Morecombe. A whole week to themselves. Mother said they stayed at a nice place, a boarding house I believe, and apparently it was a special experience.

But then they had to come back and resume their lives. She housekeeping for Aunt Bessie and the lodger in South Stainmore, and he farming over at North Stainmore. They could not live together. That's probably why they had to write to each other even after they were married. It was to be more than five years before they were able to lead a normal married life. They would spend the occasional weekend together when the chance occurred, but that's all.

Nowadays, people wouldn't put up with those circum-stances, but in those days it was accepted as a fact of life. They had to face reality and did not pine for what was not possible –

just got on with life as best they could. I know Mother used to help out at Low Fields in an attempt to ease Daddy's burden a bit.

Mother stayed with Aunt Bessie until she died. That was a bad time for her because she fell between two stools in a way. She lost her home, was apart from her own family and my father, and did not fare very well at all when the time came to divide Aunt Bessie's property. I do not think she benefited at all financially – if she did it was a very small amount – and wouldn't have been able to keep any of the furniture had it not been for the kindness of Aunt Mary. The kitchen table I have today came from Aunt Bessie, along with my rocking chair, a brass pan and some pictures. Aunt Mary made sure that Mother left with something.

It was Aunt Bessie's death, coupled with another event, which did finally bring Mother and Father together permanently. You see, Great-Uncle Isaac at Dummah Hill had a housekeeper called Eleanor Anne Cleasby and she and Uncle Tommy got married, which caused a bit of a mix-up. By that time, Uncle Tommy was living at Sleetburn in Baldersdale with his parents, my Grandfather James and Grandma Elizabeth Hauxwell, and his new wife didn't want to leave Dummah Hill. So the family agreed on a swap – Uncle Tommy would go there and Father would take over Sleetburn, which was rented from a man called William Hutchinson.

But even the happiness Mother and Father felt at being able to live together under the same roof at last was tinged with sadness, because they both liked Stainmore very much and would have preferred to stay in the area. And then they couldn't be on their own because they had the elderly relatives to care for. Of course, fate decreed that they never would.

Life at Sleetburn created other problems for Mother. She had never farmed before, and she told me that it did not come easy. I think she was twenty-eight when she learned to milk, and she said it made her knees shake.

I was born at Sleetburn, on 1 August 1926. Mother and Father had been married for six years and I was to be their only child. Dr Dawson, a wonderful man who died not long ago,

was present and my arrival had an unfortunate repercussion. Maybe it was a difficult birth – no one ever said – but Mother got up too soon because there was a lot of washing to do and contracted pleurisy. Father had to poultice her, which is what they did in those days.

I cannot recall anything about Sleetburn. My earliest memories are of Low Birk Hatt, which Daddy bought at auction when I was three, at what turned out to be an inflated price. Paying off the mortgage created difficulties when the income from the farm declined during the bad times, which was more often than not, when prices fell for our sheep, cattle and produce.

I can remember as a small child Daddy coming back from Barnard Castle with big loads on his bicycle. And there was an occasion when we were at a chapel anniversary service and Mother had to go on the platform to sing. She had a lovely contralto voice. I didn't take kindly to being parted from her and climbed up beside her.

The Depression happened when I was little, with the Jarrow march and all that dreadful unemployment and suffering. I was oblivious to it all, but I don't know how we managed, as agriculture suffered along with every other industry.

Daddy was the only able-bodied man on our farm. The elderly relatives did what they could but it meant that all through his life – not that he even survived to forty – there was never a chance to take it a bit easier, no one he could rely on to do the work if he was ill or tired. And Mother had her hands full coping with the housework and looking after four old people.

In addition to Father's parents, two bachelor uncles came to live with us at Low Birk Hatt: Great-Uncle Isaac from Dummah Hill and his younger brother, Great-Uncle William Bayles. They all became ill and infirm, which increased Mother's workload, and it was all made worse because of the lack of space. Low Birk Hatt has three bedrooms but the back

opposite, Eleanor Anne (née Cleasby), wife of Uncle Tommy Hauxwell. (The flowers in the hat are believed to be real!)

47

bedroom wasn't used very much because it had no fireplace and couldn't be heated. So Grandma and Grandad had one bedroom, Mother, Father and me slept in the other one, and the two brothers slept downstairs.

I know Mother worried a lot about the money situation, but Daddy kept a tight control on things and people in Baldersdale were very good at helping each other out. The bank was usually very understanding, and generally gave us some leeway until we were able to sell something. And a firm run by Ralph Willie Raynes, which used to supply most of our goods, would allow extended credit when it became necessary.

The pity of it was, not long after my father died in 1933 things improved quite a lot in the material sense. A grand little chap called Willie Workman was largely responsible. He lived over in Westmorland and was in the milk business, and then he met and married a Baldersdale girl, Anne Coldfield from Dill House, and they came to live here. They took over the farm at Blind Beck and Willie pioneered the collection of milk throughout the whole dale. Up until then people had made butter and sometimes cheese from the milk since there had never been a collection until Willie, who was a very good businessman, began to transport it out – on a horse and cart at first, until he acquired a wagon. It led to a vast improvement for everybody in Baldersdale because it provided a regular income. Making butter was nowhere near as reliable.

Then war broke out in 1939 and made a difference, as it always does. Farm prices inevitably improve at times like that, which is sad in one way, but it removed a lot of worries in Baldersdale. We were given subsidies on cattle and sheep as well. I don't remember hearing Mr Chamberlain announcing the outbreak of war, although we had a wireless by then. We were probably all busy out in the fields at the time since it happened at the beginning of September. The news got around, I believe, when somebody went and rang up a newspaper, probably the *Darlington and Stockton Times*, to enquire. By and large, the war passed us by in Baldersdale, although we had to go through the business of putting black- out curtains at all the windows, even though all the light we had was from oil lamps.

Nelly (seated) and Lizzie Hauxwell, Uncle Tommy's twin daughters

I think maybe half a dozen men went to war from Baldersdale, and poor Sidney Fawcett from West Birk Hatt was shot and killed while trying to escape from a prisoner-of-war camp. Sometimes I would hear conversations about the war when some of the older men in the dale came to chat and have a cup of tea in the kitchen with Uncle Tommy, who had come to take over Low Birk Hatt after Father died. Unfortunately, his marriage had broken down and he and his wife had separated. They had three children – twin girls, Lizzie and Nellie, and a son, Willie.

Uncle was quite keen on listening to the nine o'clock news and I remember hearing Mr Churchill. We got our ration books – for us and the cattle-food as well – but I don't think I ever worried about the possibility of Hitler invading us. The war was so far away and I suppose it was only in later years we learned how serious the threat was. We had other matters on our minds at the time, as it happens. Grandma Hauxwell died in December 1940, and that left just Mother, Uncle and myself. Grandad was dead by then and so were the two great-uncles. There had been rather a lot of funerals at Low Birk Hatt and they weren't inexpensive. That tended to balance out the extra income from the milk collection and the wartime subsidies, so we never really achieved the desirable state of feeling well off.

The only gunfire we heard was from the army rifle range across the hill, and sometimes they would bring tanks up on big wagons so they could practice on the moor.

The biggest excitement of the war for us happened when an aeroplane came down on the hill above Clove Lodge, which is just across the valley from Low Birk Hatt. But it was one of ours. I don't know what sort of plane it was because it was unrecognizable. It ploughed into the ground scattering debris and bits of aluminium all over the place. Friends took me up to have a closer look at it, and I understand the pilot, who was an Australian, managed to bale out and came down safely somewhere near Balder Head.

The war brought a lot of changes to Baldersdale, however. At the start, work was done by horsepower in the strict sense of the word. Then the first jeep, war surplus, came into the dale and it was cut down to turn it into more of a wagon. It was followed by the first tractors, the little grey Fergusons. They were grand machines. But Low Birk Hatt was never able to support such a luxury.

5

Bikes, Circuses… and the Wonders of the Wireless

The twentieth century arrived rather late in Baldersdale. Some corners missed part of it altogether, none more so than Low Birk Hatt. Even during the last decade before the dawn of the twenty-first century, the prospect of water on tap there was still problematical. When Hannah was a child, running water meant the stream in the field and such things as electricity, the internal combustion engine and even the wireless were available only on another planet, or so it must have seemed to the average resident of this remote and lovely, but intensely deprived valley. As she grew up, a few of these technological marvels began to slowly percolate into the Dales. Personal transport had since the dawn of time been limited to footslogging or a horse not too exhausted by its labour in the fields. But the bicycle arrived, and then the two wheels driven by a mysterious force, known as a motorbike. Far more significant and revelatory was the arrival of the wireless, in the sense that it meant for the first time the voice of the outside world and all that it encompassed – good and bad – was heard throughout this enclosed community. It encouraged Baldersdale to look up and beyond its natural boundaries. The days of innocence were over – well, almost.

We got our first wireless second-hand from John Thwaites at High Birk Hatt just before the outbreak of war in 1939. I think it cost thirty shillings. It was a Pye and a grand set it was too. John helped us to fix it, setting up the outside aerial with those little white pot things with holes in. They resembled the pot eggs you used to put under hens to encourage them to lay.

It was run on accumulator batteries which were filled with acid, and they were the big drawback. They lasted all too shortly – maybe a fortnight or so – before they needed to be recharged, and they always seemed to fade at a crucial time, in the middle of your favourite programme. But Mrs Fawcett at

West Birk Hatt had a brother, a clever man called Tommy Rayne, who could charge them. Trouble was he lived at Selsit, which was up over the Pennine Way, across the high moor, and it meant a three-hour trek there and back. Those batteries were big, heavy glass things and took some carrying, particularly on a hot day. Fortunately, we had friends at Kelton, which was on the way, about an hour's walk into the journey, so one could stop and rest. There were risks involved because the acid sometimes leaked and I ruined a couple of dresses that way. One was a very nice garment made out of a kind of silk which Mother and I bought from the secondhand clothes lady who ran a stall in Barnard Castle. Mother used some washing soda to try and get the stain out but it didn't work. I still have the dress, which only goes to prove once again how difficult I find it to throw anything away!

When we arrived at Selsit, we would exchange the flat battery for a fully charged one and walk back. The charge was sixpence – six old pence – which is 2½p today.

The wireless made such a difference to our lives. We felt less cut off from society as a whole and I was particularly pleased to be able to listen to good music on a regular basis.

Eventually we got another wireless, a Murphy I think, again second-hand, from John Thwaites. It would have been wonderful if we could have been able to afford a gramophone as well. I know Mother would have liked it because she had some experience of one when she was living with Aunt Bessie, over in Stainmore. When she was young, Aunt Bessie had been in service for a well-off family with a certain Mrs Leigh, who lived in Colne in Lancashire. Aunt Bessie used to go and stay there and take Mother along too. The Leighs worked in a cotton mill and they had a gramophone, which Mother thought was a wonderful thing. But then you couldn't just switch it on and listen to the music like the wireless. It was necessary to buy records, and that factor would have put it beyond our reach. Such a pity.

But for Uncle Tommy, I think an even bigger thrill than the arrival of the wireless was the day he acquired a motorbike. He bought it from a chap called John Dowson, who later married one of the Miss Sayers from West New Houses. I believe the sum of fifty shillings (£2.50) changed hands.

It was an Imperial and he was so proud of it, although he sometimes had considerable difficulty in making it go.

Neddy Fawcett, who was farming at West Birk Hatt in the days before it was flooded when the new reservoir opened, was very good with mechanical things and used to come over and try to make it start.

I would sometimes ride on the back to go to chapel, or shopping, and the furthest I ever went was when Uncle Tommy took me to Middleton in Teesdale to see Sir Robert Fossett's Circus. I was about ten at the time and I found it all a bit frightening. I had never seen such crowds before and when we joined the big queue to get in, some of the young people became 'up by' as we say, which means excitable. A lot of pushing and shoving went on and I panicked a bit, so Uncle picked me up in his arms to protect me and calm me down.

opposite, *Neddy (Edmund) Fawcett with wife, Meggie, and daughter, Margaret*

below, *West Birk Hatt, the remains of which are now under Baldersdale's top reservoir*

My memory of the occasion is rather vague otherwise – perhaps it was obliterated by the fear I felt. I do recall a pal of Uncle's, called Will Rayne, who was dressed in a check suit, struggling out of the crowd and sitting down somewhat red in the face from his exertions, on the tubs in the ring before the performance started. And I do believe there were some elephants, which I liked. But I can't recall much else.

The next circus I attended, still before the war started, was Bertram Mills at Darlington. Now, that was a much more orderly occasion with people waiting patiently to enter the tent instead of creating a crush. We didn't go on the motorbike that time, since Darlington was rather a long way and the general unreliability of the machine argued against using it. We walked down to Cotherstone, caught the bus and stayed the night with our relatives in Piercebridge.

An even bigger treat happened during the war when we went to Darlington again to see Big Bill Campbell and his Rocky Mountain Rhythm at the Hippodrome Theatre. Now, we never missed Big Bill's programme on the BBC if we could help it – it was just so tuneful. They were all there, including Buck Douglas and the Old Log Cabin, and the theatre was absolutely full. It was exhilarating because they were just as good in the flesh as they were on the wireless.

By that time poor Uncle had no motorbike. It was just a brief spell of ownership; the war meant petrol rationing. He did love it so. Today, when I see people on marvellous new motorbikes, just flying about and knocking them to bits, it makes me feel so sad. If he had been able to ride one of those he would have thought he was a millionaire.

I had two wheels of my own as it happens – still have, in fact. My first bike was a Hercules, which Grandma got for me from a niece of hers. Uncle tried to teach me to ride it but I didn't really become proficient because I was scared of falling off, and the area around Low Birk Hatt wasn't much good for cycling.

I never rode around bends or up steep hills. I would get off and push. Now I did once ride it to Cotherstone Show around the time I was twenty-one and going there was just fine because it was mostly downhill. But a neighbour kindly brought it back to Baldersdale for me. I think that was the last time I had a proper ride on a bike. Other traffic on the road always worried me, so I would stop and get off until the way was clear. Years later when I saw John Sayers of West New Houses for the last time before he unfortunately died, I mentioned that I was planning to start riding my bike again, and he was most amused. He knew that I had always stopped and got off if there was anything else on the road – and that was back in wartime remember – so he said that with the sort of traffic that's on the road now I would never be on for getting off!

Later on in life I did acquire another bike, a Raleigh, and a good, stout little bike it is. It was all due to the kindness of a lady, Miss Margaret Higginson, who became one of my dearest friends. She was the headmistress of a school in Bolton and read about me when Alec Donaldson wrote an article in the *Yorkshire Post*, which was the first time my name was brought to the attention of the public. Then some of her pupils walked the Pennine Way, which runs through the land around Low Birk Hatt, and she sent a message and a box of chocolates with them. Now, I am sadly lacking when it comes to corresponding, but that time I did manage to write and thank her, adding that she would always be welcome to come and call if she ever was in the area. I didn't expect her to do so, but what I didn't know then was that she had a holiday cottage in Muker, which is not far over the hills in Swaledale, and one day she turned up with some friends of hers.

By then, I hadn't got a wireless but she declared that it was an absolutely necessary thing for someone in my situation and brought me a red one, of the kind that worked on batteries – thankfully, not the kind you had to carry for miles to be recharged! And when that one 'went home' she provided me with another one, which is still going today.

One day she turned up with the Raleigh bike because she was worried that I didn't get out much. That was twenty years ago. It was some years before I actually tried to ride it, and that was all because of the kindness of Martin from Sunderland. I

The Hippodrome in Parkgate, Darlington, a generation ago
(Courtesy of Darlington Library)

am afraid I don't know his second name, but I have been his friend since he was a boy. His family used to come and stay for a week every year in a cottage across the dale and Martin would come and visit me on a regular basis. He was such a nice boy. He had a dog and, being city-bred, he thought Baldersdale was wonderful. A real place of adventure. I've seen Martin grow up. One year he arrived with a young lady, then came back when she was his wife. Then they turned up with their little son, Daniel, to introduce him to me. I suppose he will be nearly grown up now.

Well, one year when he was about seventeen, Martin arrived to sort out my bicycle. The Raleigh. I hadn't ridden one since just after the war. He oiled it, pumped up the tyres and held it for me while I had a go, just in the yard at first. Then I tried it on the pasture, but that was a bit rough, so I thought I would ride it down the new road through the iron gate leading out of my land. It has a fairly pronounced slope and a hump in the middle which proved my undoing. Twice I came off at that spot.

The experience rather put me off but I still have the Raleigh with me in Cotherstone, and keep hoping to have another go. But if I do, I will have to keep to the by-roads, because the traffic on the main road outside my cottage can be very busy in summer.

We never had perils like that in Baldersdale, so civilization can have its drawbacks. Nevertheless, I do admit relishing its other benefits, particularly water on tap. A water supply was very slow coming to Baldersdale and never did arrive at Low Birk Hatt. The only place I know which had water supplied by the Tees Valley Water Board was West Friar House, which was owned by Roy Bainbridge. Apparently, he had reserved certain rights which entitled him to a supply. Other people had to get their water from where they could, and at their own expense. Some were more fortunate than others because their land had a spring.

There was a plan once to supply our place and the Fawcetts' at West Birk Hatt from a source within the boundaries of High Birk Hatt, but the Fawcetts had to leave when their farm disappeared under the waters of Balderhead Reservoir which, ironically, put paid to that enterprise.

Uncle was still alive – but not for long – when electricity came to Baldersdale around 1961. Now that was such a big thing and caused a lot of excitement. A few places further down the dale had got it at once, and then it began to advance further up towards us. The electricity people called to ask my permission to put poles in my land so that they could take it even higher, and I agreed to it. But I don't think I ever seriously considered having Low Birk Hatt connected when they offered it to me. It was the expense, you see. It just was not possible.

6

Leaping Preachers, Soporific Sermons and the Art of Muck Spreading

For more than a hundred years throughout the Dales of Yorkshire, the pivot of community life, the one platform for self-expression open to everyone, was the chapel. It had a virtual monopoly on social life, organizing the annual outings, sports days, tea parties and concerts which were the highlights of the year in an era which was starved of communication and leisure and wearied by the constant treadmill of work on the land. During Hannah's childhood and well beyond, Dalesfolk lived in a closed world where to travel more than a dozen miles from the farmstead was an unusual adventure, the wireless a strange and suspicious device from foreign parts and a local newspaper something of an occasional luxury.

The less formalized form of religion brought to the Dales by John Wesley and his brother suited the collective personality of these people perfectly. For a long time there had been a struggle for supremacy between the established church, the Quakers, the Catholics and the Congregationalists. The spiritual history of Cotherstone reflects the ebb and flow of religious influence in the Teesdale area. George Fox arrived there in 1653 and established the Quakers as the dominant force in the village. The next village just down the road, Lartington, stayed loyal to the Church of Rome, which led to a spot of tension now and then. The Church of England established their place of worship in 1796, then built St Cuthbert's in 1881 and a school in 1894. The Congregationalists arrived in 1869, but the balance of power shifted to the Methodists around 1874. They, too, added a school to their chapel and the Wesleyan message spread swiftly into the more remote corners – the far-flung network of small and isolated communities like Baldersdale.

The heat of battle has died away now. Both the Methodist and Church of England schools in Cotherstone have been replaced by a state school (the Methodists hung on until 1960). But it is still generally recognized as a Methodist village, and Hannah is

62

counted among the worshippers at the chapel who are, in the main, elderly. But when Hannah was a girl, chapel was a place for the young and energetic, for people who wanted their voices to be heard. Life in those days offered few opportunities for young men and women with ambition. But one way of making your mark was to become a preacher.

My goodness, we certainly did have some outstandingly good preachers around these parts, particularly before the war. Sometimes, whole families of them, like the Beadles of Upper Teesdale who were familiar faces in Methodist pulpits. There were three brothers, Jacob, Phillip and John, who were very much their own men and who would stick to a viewpoint through thick and thin. They were marvellous speakers, even though I understand they did not have the benefit of what was considered an education.

Rather strenuous debates on religious issues were quite commonplace and Uncle Tommy was always ready to take part. He knew the Beadles well – they were very forceful and witty and Uncle would have many a fierce but friendly argument with them. I think maybe he didn't share some of their more extreme views.

Mind, Uncle could be just as witty as them sometimes. There was one occasion when he was in discussion with Jacob Beadle, a very strong, good-looking man, and the topic was muck spreading. In those days, the manure was distributed on the fields in heaps from a horse and cart and then you would have to follow behind with a handfork to rake it and spread it evenly. It's a task I am well familiar with myself.

Anyway, Jacob said that he could do the job better and more quickly if he paced himself by singing a lively hymn called 'Keep in Step with the Master'. Uncle replied that Jacob's choice was no good for him. His own particular selection for the job was the much slower 'Art Thou Weary, Art Thou Languid'!

Uncle did some preaching too, in and around the Teesdale area, but I never went to hear him. It would have been embarrassing for me. I did listen to him proposing a vote of

A parade of Methodist preachers active in Teesdale, taken in 1948

Uncle Tommy in later years – centre, with white hair, glasses and left hand on chin

thanks occasionally, and I was always glad when he sat down.

Some of the preachers used to be very enthusiastic, not to say a trifle over-active, when delivering their message. Uncle used to tell the story about one of the fiery kind, a real character, who delivered a sermon one Sunday in a chapel with an unusually long pulpit. As the sermon wore on and he became more and more excited, he began to jump from one side, first to the middle and, by the time he was in full verbal flight, he managed to leap the entire length of the pulpit. The congregation was mesmerized.

I have vivid memories of several preachers who came to

Baldersdale, particularly one evangelist called Rhoda Dent. It was quite unusual in those days for a woman to become a preacher, but she was very good and most eloquent. She came from a family that lived on North Stainmore, where my father was raised, and she had striking looks. She was well built, with strong features, and she styled her dark brown hair in what they called earphones. You needed to have a good, full, thick crop of hair to plait in order to achieve this effect, and I thought it nice.

On one occasion she held a mission at the Methodist chapel in Baldersdale which went on every night for two weeks. People came from many other local chapels to attend, which meant quite an effort in those days when very few people had cars. People mostly walked or came on bicycles. Some of those services used to build up a wonderful feeling, and now and then it would become rather emotional with the preacher calling on folk to come forward to the penitents' bench at the front to re-dedicate their lives to the Lord.

Rhoda Annie Dent was her full name and I understand she was once invited to speak on the *Queen Mary* during one voyage. In later years she went to Leeds and married a minister. She kindly wrote me a letter after the first television programme about me, since her family and mine had been friends for years. Her father, Ralph Dent, a somewhat excitable fellow, was a pal of Uncle's and they used to have many animated discussions about different aspects of religion. Rhoda had a brother called Tom, a very pleasant young man who also became a preacher, but not for long because, unfortunately, he died young.

Another preacher who made an impression locally was an Irishman called John Wesley Kingston. He once held a mission in Romaldkirk which I attended. He was a fairly good-looking young man and I do believe he came on the recommendation of Rhoda. He wrote a book which we bought, all about the discrimination he endured as a Methodist living in Ireland.

Personally, I didn't care a lot at all for the more dramatic kind of preachers, those who would shout and thump the

John Wesley Kingston, Irish evangelist

opposite, *Rhoda Dent, taken c. 1930*

pulpit. It is perfectly possible to get your message across without being so histrionic. And those sermons, they did carry on so. It was particularly hard to bear when one was a child. You would think that they were – thankfully – drawing to a close, and then they would burst off again for another hour and you found yourself wishing they would just shut up.

I know that nowadays the congregations at chapels have sadly declined but if the services lasted as long today as they did in my childhood they would be empty altogether.

Some of those involved had quite a critical, holier-than-thou approach. I recall one occasion when Mother was so busy trying to finish knitting a quilt – I've still got it somewhere – that she said she would have to miss a service. They were having a mission at the time and the preacher told Mother that it would have done her far more good to go to chapel than knit a quilt. Mother wasn't moved at all.

Uncle used to tell me about the time when the Primitive Methodists and the Wesley Methodists were joining up. This created a lot of controversy and gave those who were fond of the sound of their own voices an unrivalled opportunity. They used to have what they called 'quarterly meetings', where the various stewards would render reports and accounts. They were always verbal marathons. No, those long-winded gentlemen put me off sermons for a good long while. And then, of course, I wasn't able to attend much when I was left on my own after Mother and Uncle Tommy died and I had all the milking and farmwork to do myself.

When Grandmother was alive, I would go to the church services held in the schoolroom in Baldersdale because Grandma was Church of England. Mother used to come too, although she was chapel, and then we would go on to the Methodist service in the evening. Although I was baptized into the Methodist faith I used to prefer the church service because it didn't go on so long. Mind, I do worry about the Church of England because of its beginnings and its association with Henry VIII. He is not a character I like at all because I think he was just an old rascal. You hear about the times of good King Hal, and the rather implausible suggestion that he wrote 'Greensleeves', but I don't see him in any romantic light at all. I am just glad I wasn't Anne Boleyn, or some other lady who took his fancy.

Now, as far as the Catholics are concerned, I have to say I like the people very much but theirs is not a faith I could accept myself. I know things have altered recently, but certainly at one time you couldn't speak to God yourself and confess your sins direct to Him. You had to do it through a priest. Neither am I happy about the ceremony and the burning of incense. Then there is the question of the nuns and monks entering one or other of the orders where they become prisoners, more or less. To me that seems intolerable. I know people have written saying that I look like a nun, or could have been a nun, but that's the last thing I would want to be. Life must be free to do what one wishes and, to a certain point, to say what one wishes. To have to do what someone else says, and to be behind bolted doors is just unacceptable to me.

The reason I prefer the Methodist faith is because it has the simplest form. They also have the best hymns, good old jolly tunes. I can be far more moved by music than any sermon. I mean, take Beethoven's 'Pastoral' Symphony. If there is anything capable of lifting you up to the gates of heaven, then that is it.

Now, I must stress that Christianity is very important to me, although maybe I am not deeply religious or believe enough. One hopes there is a heaven where one will meet up with one's loved ones but I don't know. That's why I look upon death as a horrible thing – it seems so final. We don't know what's on the other side, if anything. I just cannot blindly believe that we move out of this life and enter into a better one.

Nor do I believe that to be a good Christian you have to attend chapel or church every week, or even three times a year. The most important thing is how people live. There are a lot of good people who may never enter a place of worship. But I do go to the Methodist Chapel in Cotherstone as often as I can and, now and again, support various chapel functions in other places when asked. I even made an appearance at a big Salvation Army event in Sheffield one weekend.

And I have met the man who is probably the best-known preacher in the world today, Dr Billy Graham. He was a guest on the first *Wogan* show I appeared on. We stood together in the entrance hall of the theatre where the show is produced, but I have to confess that I didn't recognize him. Later, we met very briefly. We couldn't talk because I believe he badly wanted to telephone someone who had just returned from China, so it was just a handshake really. Not a conversation, but a very good handshake. Still, I liked him, and I have heard him on television once or twice. And when you think he is in his seventies and working so hard night after night, you have to admire him.

Not long after meeting him I went on a bus trip to a rally

Billy Graham on the Wogan *show* (Courtesy of Russ Busby)

held in a big place where they had an enormous screen with Billy Graham appearing by satellite. There were such a lot of people there. In fact, it was full – which I didn't like very much because I am nervous in crowds. But the organ music was lovely, although some of the vocalists sang rather modern stuff, a bit like rock and roll. I'm not so keen on that but I know that they have to attract young people as well.

Dr Graham was, as you might expect, most eloquent and, when he appealed for people to come forward and dedicate themselves, quite a few got up and went towards the screen just as though he was really there. Of course, there were people positioned to receive them.

But I didn't go. In fact the room was so warm, and I have this tired feeling such a lot these days, that I'm afraid I fell asleep!

7

The Gentry: Beating for Grouse and the 'Slavery' of the Hiring Fair

Baldersdale was far too remote for any of the gentry to be interested in building a country residence there. All the more accessible dales had their halls, manors and castles, but the high moors sweeping up to 1,500 feet above the valley of Baldersdale was the habitat of a creature which every aristocrat, and many wealthy merchants and other *nouveau riche* with aristocratic pretentions pursued, then and now, with fanatical zeal – *Lagopus scoticus*, feathered-footed member of the Tetraonidae family, otherwise known as the red grouse. For the locals it meant an extra cash crop during the days following the Glorious Twelfth – the shillings and sovereigns tossed, somewhat disdainfully, at them for providing a back-up service, such as beating the heather to alarm the birds into the air and towards the buckshot, or placing their horses and wagons at the disposal of their lordships so that ammunition, lunch and the essential bottles of whisky could be transported to the guns and the day's bag of slain birds brought safely to the all-important count. For centuries the continual struggle of ordinary country-folk to harvest an income to keep them and their families above starvation level meant that they were always prepared to swallow their pride and go, cap in hand, to the gentry for a few vital coppers. The same philosophy spawned the hiring fairs (which continued until the second half of the century) when the 'spare' children of rural (and sometimes urban) families, not required for work at home, were sent to stand at appointed places where prospective employers could examine and inter-rogate them, checking their limbs for strength and making sure they were properly subservient. There wasn't a deal of dif-ference, fundamentally, between hiring fairs (as immortalized by Thomas Hardy in *Far From the Madding Crowd*) and the weekly cattle auctions held in market towns.

Hannah, and some of her friends in Baldersdale, have vivid recollections of the gentry and their ways, and personal experience of accepting the 'God's Penny' and going into service.

Leading Business Men Of The West Riding.

Sir Emmanuel Hoyle, of Huddersfield. Governing director of Joseph Hoyle and Son, Ltd., Prospect Mills, Longwood, Huddersfield. Four years ago, more out of sentiment than anything else, purchased Portland Mills, Lindley, where his father, the late Mr. Joseph Hoyle, the founder, first began business. Is a firm believer in the idea that a principal can be his own best traveller, and has made several long voyages on business, on one of which he visited 27 countries and got orders in many of them. A fine type of sportsman, Sir Emmanuel has been prominently interested in the Turf, aviation, shooting, athletics, and football, as well as motor-racing. For some years was president of the Huddersfield C. and A.C.; now president of the Huddersfield Town Club. Past-president also of the Northern Counties' Athletic Association, was Northern Representative on the A.A.A., and has often acted as a judge and referee. Well known as an owner on the Turf, one of the first in this country to own a private aeroplane, and winner of many road-racing and hill-climbing contests. Some years ago became Conservative candidate for Darwen, but retired before the election owing to ill-health. Became a Knight of the British Empire shortly after the war, was knighted in 1922, and made a justice of the peace for the borough of Huddersfield in November, 1920.

Sir Emmanuel Hoyle, Master of mill and moor

Sir Emmanuel Hoyle owned the shooting rights in these parts. He came from Yorkshire, I believe, where he owned a mill and he could be quite a difficult man. I never met him and, after what I heard about him, I never had any ambition so to do. Uncle Tommy, along with the Fawcetts and John Thwaites from High Birk Hatt, used to work for him during the grouse season. They were nice takings you see, a bit extra, which was very welcome.

Uncle rented out our horse and cart to carry the lunch-baskets and the cartridges and to collect the bag at the end of the day. He said you could always tell first thing what sort of mood Sir Emmanuel was in. If he said 'Good morning, men!' as he passed by then it might not be such a bad day. But if he went stomping by without saying anything it was a clear indication of trouble ahead. Apparently, on one occasion, as he stormed past Uncle and Sam Fawcett, Uncle told Sam that someone was sure to cop it before the day was out. And it turned out to be them.

Sir Emmanuel had a florid complexion which, apparently, became redder and redder as his temper grew worse, and his language was appalling. Sam's brother, Neddy, incurred his wrath one day as he was driving the birds down towards the guns. He was the official gamekeeper and knew the job inside out but for some reason what he was doing didn't suit Sir Emmanuel and the air turned blue. And there was a bonny pantomime once when a couple of grouse went missing and Uncle and Sam got into trouble. They had been so busy collecting the birds and tying them up. Completely innocent they were, too, but it made no difference.

Still, Sir Emmanuel had the money. He was paying the piper.

The Thwaites at High Birk Hatt farmed alongside the Hauxwells, and John Thwaites worked with Uncle Tommy and the Fawcetts for Sir Emmanuel. John and his wife Marie live in retirement nowadays not far from Cotherstone and they actually cut short their honeymoon in order not to miss the shoot.

Aye, but you must remember that money was so scarce in the thirties that you couldn't miss anything. Marie and me were on our honeymoon, staying with my brother in Darlington, when I got this letter from my mother saying we must come back immediately because they were starting the shoot. You see, I had just graduated to the position of providing a horse and cart, and any amount of people wanted that job so I would have lost it, maybe for good, if I hadn't turned up.

The pay was fifteen shillings a day then, and that was for the horse, cart and man. An ordinary beater got five shillings. That was a lot of money in those days and there were a lot of men eager to do it – around twenty or thirty out of Baldersdale were hired. The shoot used to last five or six days in August but you didn't get paid when it was finished – don't ask me why, but we had to wait until Christmas. Later on, I believe, the pay went up to a pound or even twenty-five shillings for a man, horse and cart.

So we came back from honeymoon three or four days early. But Marie understood. My job was to take the cart up on the moor to a place called Mile End, and you sat with it all day until they brought the grouse to you.

Sir Emmanuel had a terrible bad temper and was often full of whisky. Most of his guests drank a lot, including some of the younger gentlemen. I particularly remember old Hoyle's solicitor, a great fat, brewsy fella from Leeds who drank whisky like a duck. And you had to be very careful with the grouse. When I first started on the shoot, Sam Fawcett said that I needn't bother about the whisky and the cartridges but I had to watch the grouse, and not to let anyone come past them and pick one or two out. Losing a grouse was the sin of sins. I never did lose any at all, but a couple did go missing one day and there was hell to pay.

George Fawcett, one of Sam's sons and now in his seventies, also has keen recall of his boyhood days working as a beater under his father's orders. Sir Emmanuel, as the owner of West Birk Hatt, was the Fawcetts' landlord.

Sir Emmanuel's men – the beaters and loaders from Baldersdale

The first drive I went on made me wonder about the sanity of grouse. The guns were blazing away at them but they just kept coming. Any other bird would have flown the other way. They could see their pals being shot down in front of them but it made no difference. They were daft birds, stupid. And some of Sir Emmanuel's guests were a bit that way, too. You were only supposed to take the birds directly before you, not follow them sideways because that meant the man in the next butt could come within range. Several times they ended up shooting each other. One day, an American guest became a bit too enthusiastic, aimed all over the place and ended up peppering several others, I believe. Father got it more than once over the years. One pellet lodged between his eyes and became a permanent dimple.

Sir Emmanuel was a fair shot and, on a good day, there would be three or four hundred brace to bring back. Once, the count topped five hundred brace – one thousand birds – but that was an exceptional day.

All the grouse used to be brought to my dad, who was awful particular about displaying them. We had a large table and Dad would lay them out in rows to cool, tuck their heads under their wings and put pieces of heather in between them. Damaged birds would be sewn up by Mother and their feathers ruffled to look nice. At the end of the day, they would all be taken down to Romaldkirk and put on a train, although on one occasion Sir Emmanuel had his private aeroplane sent up to transport them.

Mother used to make a big meal to feed the beaters when they came to unload and help pack the grouse, but the food for the gentry was taken to the moor in large hampers. They had a wooden hut built up there especially to have their lunch in, and there would be plenty to drink, including a hogshead of beer.

I know they are supposed to be a delicacy but none of our family liked to eat grouse. Some of the older birds could be very tough. Mahogany Joes, we used to call them, and there was a sure method of finding out if a grouse was getting on a bit. You put a bit of pressure on its mandible, or lower beak,

Hannah outside her new home, Belle Vue Cottage, Cotherstone

above, *The main bedroom*

below, *'I'm like a child when it comes to running water'*

above, *Hannah's new friend, the telephone. It's an ex-directory number or it would never rest*

below, *The mail continues to pour in, from more than one continent*

above, *An afternoon chat with friends, Mrs Annie Bousfield and Mrs Hannah Iceston, on the village green*

below, *Hair like spun silk, backlit outside one of the village pubs*

above, *Off to collect her pension at Cotherstone Post Office*

below, *Checking the prices in the window of Kelvin Walker's shop*

above, *A classic Teesdale hay meadow*

below, *The 'Flower Man', Mike Prosser, relaxing by a stream*

Adder's-tongue fern
(Ophioglossum vulgatum)

Moonwort (Botrychium lunaria)

Frog orchid (Coeloglossum viricle)

Geranium sylvaticum

Lady's mantle (Alchemilla)

The 'Hannah Hauxwell' Rose

In 1989 Hannah achieved a long-held ambition when a new friend, Mrs Nancy Smith, who has a farm in Stokesley, took her to Stokesley Show – an event which usually merits two full pages of text and pictures in the *Darlington Times and Echo* which are always read with deep interest by Hannah, who loves flowers, particularly roses.

Exhibiting at the Show was a rose-grower called Eric Stainthorpe, who had 'invented' a new rose – quite by accident. He had been cultivating a strain of 'Sweet Dreams', the variety which had been selected as the Rose of the Year in 1988. One day he noticed that a mutation of this rose, pink in colour, had emerged naturally, and he set to work to make sure it did not revert – and succeeded. The rose was still unnamed when he was introduced to Hannah at Stokesley Show. 'Oddly enough,' says Mr Stainthorpe, 'I had three names in mind: "Herriot Country", "Hadrian's Wall", or "Hannah Hauxwell". I have long been an admirer of Hannah, and I have read the books and seen the television programmes. But when I met her and shook her hand I had a feeling which is hard to explain – other people have had the same experience when meeting this lady. I felt so very humble. I knew immediately what I wanted to call the rose, and asked her there and then. She was obviously pleased to accept and I presented her with a basket of roses to celebrate.'

The 'Hannah Hauxwell' rose is a shell-pink patio rose and was officially launched at the Gateshead Show in the summer of 1990. Hannah was the guest of honour and presented the prizes.

and if it broke it was a young bird. If it didn't, it was a Mahogany Joe. Sir Emmanuel once sent us some grouse from his own table but it was not to our taste – it had been cooked in port wine and laced with some spices.

Sir Emmanuel was not an easy man to work for and you had to watch what you said. If any of the beaters did incur his wrath, they were sent home. One day a lad called Stanley Wallace created a real stir. I think he had been listening to some people in the dale who had missed out on the shoot and the money that went with it, and were critical, or pretended to be critical, of people who worked for Sir Emmanuel and the other toffs – maybe a bit left wing, although Stanley wasn't a person who took any interest in politics. Anyway, he was standing near to Sir Emmanuel, who was shooting from his butt, and a bird went down in front of the guns. Sir Emmanuel told him to go and pick it up, but Stanley replied, 'Go and pick it up yourself!' That caused a tirade, naturally, and instructions were given that the man must not be hired again.

The other event that I remember well was when my Uncle Ned could have made himself a bit of money when a bird was shot down in mistake for a grouse. Sir Emmanuel asked Uncle Ned what it was and he said it was a young cuckoo. But Sir Emmanuel was certain it was a hawk of some kind and offered to bet Uncle Ned fifty pounds that it wasn't a cuckoo. The bird was sent off to be identified by a taxidermist and Uncle turned out to be right. Unfortunately, he had refused to take the bet since it was a heck of a lot of money in those days, was fifty quid. But Sir Emmanuel was good in other ways and he used to buy our wool at a fair price. A solicitor friend of his who came on one of the shoots did a big favour for one of the beaters. He noticed that the man was missing one eye and asked him how he had lost it. The beater said it had happened years ago in a quarrying accident. The solicitor declared that he should get compensation for that, took his case on, and the man ended up with £250.

At the end of every shoot Sir Emmanuel would give a big dinner for the beaters at the Fox and Hounds in Cotherstone. It was always a good do. Hannah's grandfather, James

On the grouse moor – sorting the day's bag

Hauxwell, was invariably invited although he didn't take part in the drive. He came because he could recite poems, particularly Rudyard Kipling, and at great length. He could do one poem with sixty verses without pause, and Sir Emmanuel would listen and marvel at his ability.

Subservience was expected by all levels of employer, titled or otherwise, and Marie Thwaites was one of a number of young men and women who were packed off to a life which was not only unacceptable by today's standards, but hardly believable. Hannah Hauxwell met several who were in service in and around the Baldersdale area.

I used to see them when it was the custom for young folk to gather at Cotherstone village at weekends, to chat and meet their friends. Lads and lassies who were newly hired locally would be readily accepted when they turned up, looking for a bit of company and conversation. I well remember a young man who aroused special interest one weekend because he had been taken on at a place which had a certain reputation. When he was asked how he was getting on there he replied, 'Oh, it's like heaven.' Well, no one could make that out, but it transpired that the lad had a sense of humour. 'Yes,' he said. 'It's like the Bible says – there's no night there. We just work all the way through.'

Some people did expect an awful lot from those youngsters for the few shillings they paid them. There were no set hours, no union to look after their interests and they were lucky to get out on a Saturday or Sunday to go to the chapel, or on certain special occasions to the cinema. The lucky ones had bikes but most had to walk long distances to meet up with their friends. But at busy occasions such as haytime, they didn't get any time to themselves at all.

Not all places treated them roughly though. Over at East New Houses in Baldersdale the youngsters they hired were regarded as family. They had to pull their weight, but they brought up one or two who had lost their parents just as if they were their own children. They ended up getting married from East New Houses, with all the affection and ceremony you would give to your own child. My half-cousin Norman Bayles was hired over in Ravenstonedale and he liked it there. He was very interested in music and singing and would always be dashing off somewhere on his bicycle – later on, I believe he managed to acquire a motorbike – to practices and concerts.

The people at the farm he was hired to were very sympathetic but he still had all his work to do before he could get away. I know he was once asked to sing with a choir at the Kendal Festival of Music when Sir Adrian Boult appeared. But he had so much to do before he could leave, the milking and so on, and what with the long journey as well, he was very tired when he arrived and apparently nodded off. It seems Sir Adrian spotted him and shouted out: 'Oy – you at the back there! Wake up!'

Norman's music teacher badly wanted him to become a professional because he had a fine tenor voice and was a talented violinist. But there just wasn't the money available. Poor man, he died in 1989, just short of his eightieth birthday.

I know Marie Thwaites was in service at the time she was courting John. I liked her from the moment I met her, and I well recall the occasion – I had turned up at their place and she appeared in the yard from the shed carrying buckets of milk. Very cheerful and friendly she was then, and always has been.

Marie Thwaites has a sunny disposition, rarely stops smiling and has happy memories of her experiences as a hired hand. She considers herself one of the fortunate ones, although her innocent description of the daily regime she had to endure would be considered intolerable, indeed cruel, today. But the deprivation of her early childhood in the depressed North East does explain a lot.

I was brought up in a pit village near Bishop Auckland and I never knew my father. He was a miner and he went off to the First World War and got killed. I only knew my mother and grandmother and life was not easy – we often went hungry. When I was a schoolgirl some friends took me on to a farm and I used to watch the milking and think what a grand life it was, so healthy, not at all like life in the pits and the factories. By the time I was fourteen I couldn't wait to get away from that place and my mother took me to the hiring fair in the marketplace in Bishop Auckland. The year was 1931 and there were a lot of other lads and lassies standing around anxiously like me. All the farmers stood apart in groups, looking around. Anyway, this man came up to where I was standing with my mother, and asked if I was for hire. I said yes, that I wanted a farm place, and he asked me if I had any experience. I told him that I had watched cows being milked – that was all – but I liked the look of it. He must have liked the look of me because after a bit more discussion he said, 'Well, we'll have to learn you to milk, and learn you to feed calves and the rest will follow on. Here's your God's Penny'. Then he gave me half a crown. I nearly fell through the floor because I didn't know what owning such a lot of money was like before.

He was called Walter Dowson and a real gentleman he was. And his wife was a real lady. They had such nice manners and treated me like one of their own, so I reckon I was one of the lucky ones. Their farm, West Park, was in Lunedale and I travelled by train to Middleton in Teesdale. I was a bit lost because I had never been anywhere before, but I was met in a pony and trap and taken to my new employer. And I found I had a room all to myself. They had two children, a girl of five and a boy of two, and one of my first jobs was to take the little girl to school.

The week started at around six on a Monday morning – washday. First, I would clean the fireside, get the fire going, put a clean cloth on the table and lay it for breakfast. Next, I

Mr and Mrs Walter Dowson

had to get the cows in although there was usually a hired lad to help, and start the milking. I couldn't do that properly at first, but Mr Dowson came to show me how, telling me to pull a lot harder. The calves were to feed then, and the milk put through the separator to take the cream off. Back in the house I would start the housework until Mrs Dowson served the breakfast at around 8.30 a.m. She usually cooked bacon in the oven and there was an egg apiece, fresh from the hens on the farm. Well, I had never tasted anything so good in all my life!

After the breakfast things had been washed up I had to take the milk separator to bits and wash each part and dry them in front of the fire and then put them together again ready for the night's milking. The main housework followed, and all the oilcloth floors had to be scrubbed – houses that had oilcloth in those days were supposed to be well off. The only carpet was in the best room, or the visitors' room as they called it.

We had roast meat once a week on Sundays, served at noon on the dot, usually their own home-killed sheep or pork. It would have to last cold for most of the week, with a bit of bacon in between. But every day we would have a pudding, rice or suet, and always different.

The Dowsons' place was known as a good meat shop. I knew of one farm where they served the suet and gravy first so as to take the edge off their hunger and save the meat.

On Monday afternoons there was the ironing to do and, on other days, the cleaning and scrubbing. There were no detergents or soap powders, just washing soda that came in pellets and was used for everything, including the floors and the clothes. Then we had to grind best white sandstone to powder and scour all the top surfaces, including the ceilings. That stuff made everything beautiful. We used a tin of powder, a damp cloth and plenty of energy.

After tea at 4.00 p.m. – usually apple pie – there was the milking to do again and then we would settle down to patching, mending and darning, and making rug mats. Every year we would have to finish two mats. Well, there wasn't much else to do in the evening until one day Mr Dowson arrived and said to me and Mrs Dowson: 'Now then, I've got

In service – Marie Thwaites, aged seventeen

something for you lassies', and brought in a wireless set. It was great. The year, I think, was 1936.

They paid me five shillings a week, which was a lot more than most got. I heard the story of a lad, from the Bishop Auckland area like me, who worked at a farm in Teesdale for two shillings and sixpence a week. But the time came when he reached the age when the farmer had to pay sixpence a week for his insurance stamp, and he was sent back home because the man said he couldn't afford it. After a while, the lad turned up back at the farm and offered to work for two shillings and pay his own insurance stamp. When he'd arrived home there had been nothing to eat and not even a bed of his own. That's how it was for lots of families in those days.

Anyway, I had enough to save up to buy a Raleigh bike – one pound it cost – which meant I could cycle over to Middleton in Teesdale on my night off. There was a little shop there run by a Mr Nixon who would stay open all hours for the hired lads and lassies. The best part was his clog-repair service. I always wore clogs, and if an iron came off while I was cycling to town I could take it to him, go off somewhere like the pictures, and it would be ready and waiting for me straight afterwards. And he only charged sixpence. He also stocked bulbs and batteries for bike lamps, all kinds of useful things.

I will always maintain that I had a good time in service, and from what I heard there weren't many bad places in the Teesdale area – just the odd one here and there. But they said that it was a different matter over in the west, around Appleby way, where they generally paid more money but worked you very hard and gave you little meat. They told some awful stories about going hungry, no privileges, putting the fire out at six o'clock at night. In winter it got so cold that you would have to wear your clothes in bed.

No, I was well treated, although the hours were long.

I just got Saturday and Sunday nights off, and it would be chapel on a Sunday of course. There was a general rule that lads could stay out until ten o'clock on their night off, but lassies had to be back at 9.30 p.m. Before I got my bike that was a problem, because there was a distance of three miles from Middleton in Teesdale to the farm. You could get an extension, if you asked permission, on Saturday nights for a special occasion such as a dance, and then I met John at the carnival in Middleton. The bike came in very handy then because it's about nine miles to Cotherstone, where we used to meet.

Once or twice a year I would go home for a weekend to see my mother. I even got a job for one of my half-sisters at a place in Lunedale, but she didn't settle to the job like me and wanted to go home after a short while. But another sister followed me at the Dowsons when I left to get married.

After the wedding I came to live in Baldersdale, at the next farm to Hannah. We got on well from the moment we met and we still see each other from time to time, and talk for hours about the good old days.

8

*Adder's Tongue, Moonwort
and Frog Orchid:
the Legacy of the Hauxwells*

In the summer of 1987 a curious figure could be seen roaming the upper reaches of Baldersdale, dressed in wet-weather gear, festooned with notebooks, large-scale maps and a magnifying glass, and peering intensely over the dry-stone walls. Clearly not your average Pennine Way walker, he was, in fact, a botanist called Mike Prosser, who had been contracted by the Nature Conservancy Council to survey the area for species of rare plants and flowers which are known to flourish in certain areas of Teesdale – given the right, exceedingly rare conditions. He fell into a lively discussion with one of Hannah's neighbours which was the precursor of an important ecological event. Mike Prosser vividly recalls the occasion.

The gentleman in question did exhibit a certain alarm because when I told him why I was looking at his land he thought it might lead to a conservation order being slapped on it. He urged me to look elsewhere – particularly in the fields owned by an old lady at the next farm called Low Birk Hatt, because they were far more colourful than his. So I did as he suggested and began to walk through her land towards the farmhouse. As I walked and as I looked, I experienced what birdwatchers call a 'jizz', the feeling they get when they spot something very out of the ordinary. You could call it the Eureka factor. Certainly, I knew I had found something special.

I have to admit I had never heard of Hannah Hauxwell – well, you see, I do not possess a television set. I found her by the side of the house with her dog, looking like a complete tramp, with a patched-up old coat and hair all over the place. I had been told she was a trifle eccentric, and there she was, busily washing scores and scores of empty jam jars in two buckets of water. She was obviously the only person around, so I introduced myself and told her what my mission was. At first, I did most of the talking, and I remember asking her name, which she said was Hannah Hauxwell. When I enquired if it was Miss or Mrs Hauxwell, she said, 'Oh no, no, no – Miss by name and Miss by nature, that's what my uncle always said'. Then she gradually took over the conversation, talking about her parents and the farm, saying she knew she was old-fashioned and some people laughed at the way she farmed, but she was happy with her methods and she liked the animals. Inside the farmhouse, she showed me some of her furniture and when I saw all the cards around the place and she began to talk about how proud she was about the large number of people who wrote to her, it dawned on me that she must be a bit of a celebrity. I thought she might have been the subject of a newspaper article or something like that, but it wasn't until later that I found out just how famous she was. She was quite happy to let me do my survey and eventually I had to make my excuses or she would have gone on chatting all day.

Hannah also recalls this meeting, which was to have a most satisfying outcome. She was surprised to learn that her meadows contained so much of ecological value and was somewhat confused at first when Mike Prosser turned up that day.

I had what I refer to as the Flower Gentleman come to call on me – I'm terrible at remembering names – and I liked him at once. It came as a surprise to learn that my pasture was so interesting to him, and I should be ashamed, being a countrywoman, of being so ignorant about the plant-life around here. I used to look at things and think how bonny some of the wild flowers were – what nice colours – but I was never aware of their variety or rarity. When I was a child there was a damp place in the long meadow where there used to be a lovely yellow flower we call butterballs, and children would bring them for the teacher. There was one I used to pick in another field years ago, a purple flower with pretty leaves which sometimes turned all colours, but I never knew its name.

I suppose such things were happy on our land because we never put chemical fertilizers on it. When we got the Hill Farm

Subsidy and we were obliged to spend a certain part of it in putting something back in the soil, uncle liked Middleton Lime, so he spread a bit of that around along with basic slag, and cow manure, of course. All natural things. But I didn't do anything like that after Uncle died in 1961, so that means my land has had nothing but cow manure for twenty-five years.

So it was all a happy accident really.

I did notice, however, that some of the wild plants and flowers that seemed to do well on my pastures didn't grow in other people's fields. Mind, I have always appreciated wildlife, even if I was unaware of the names or importance in the ecological sense, and it was also apparent that our farm attracted some lovely butterflies, particularly on warm days.

I used to enjoy the bird-life, too. Some very pretty specimens used to come into our garden and perch on the windowsills but I don't know what kind of birds they were. I've seen a heron standing on one leg, and I particularly liked the owls which used to shout from our trees to their friends across the valley at Clove Lodge. I even met one in the walnut tree when I was working in the garden one night.

I am delighted at the result of the Flower Gentleman's visit.

The Flower Gentleman in question, after setting about his detailed survey following that memorable first meeting with Hannah, quickly brought in a team from the Nature Conservancy Council to confirm his findings. The Durham Wildlife Trust was alerted and their bid for the main portion of Hannah's pastures won the day. An appeal for £25,000 was launched and the money came in so rapidly that the fund was over-subscribed within a couple of months. The World Wildlife Fund chipped in with a generous sum, and one lady donated £4,000. It is more than likely that the association with Hannah Hauxwell has something to do with the spectacular success of the appeal. The fields will be named after her, and a suitably inscribed plaque installed.

But no one has more reason to feel satisfaction at the turn of events than the quiet and modest Flower Gentleman, Mike Prosser.

It took less than ten minutes to register how rich and distinctive Hannah's land was – possibly the least improved meadows in upland Durham in fact. And by 'least improved' I mean untouched by artificial fertilizers or reseeding. Also, it had certainly not been ploughed this century, if at all.

There are some special aspects to the ecological makeup of the Teesdale area unknown elsewhere, which are rooted in the ice age. There is no simple explanation, but there are two main threads. Firstly, the altitude and harsh weather in the winter meant Teesdale was not good for tree regeneration, so it is one of the few areas in England and Wales which never became deeply forested. It has remained a type of upland grass area since the recovery of vegetation after the last ice age, ten or eleven thousand years ago. The other strand concerns the local geological history. Whereas fairly large areas in the Yorkshire Dales and up to the Scottish Borders were not heavily forested, the Teesdale region had this peculiar sugar limestone, creating a very thin, calcium-rich soil which never produced dense grass cover. But other plants were allowed to develop because the unusual chemical composition of the soil did not allow aggressive species to take over. This led to an enormous diversity of plants, none of them doing particularly well and none taken out by trees. Once you get a fertile soil, the bully boys tend to take over and only about half a dozen plants flourish. So Teesdale has a tremendously rich flora – indeed, some people think that many of the species are ice-age relics, which were there before and managed to hang on. The seeds of some of them may be millions of years old.

For these plants to survive, even in these beneficial conditions, it is necessary to have traditionally managed hay meadows. They were once very common in Teesdale and its tributary dales, like Baldersdale, but with the coming of intensive farming the picture changed dramatically. There was increased reseeding and cutting for silage, which entails heavy fertilization of the grass so that it grows very quickly to give you an early crop, then putting in more fertilizer to enable you to cut it again. Sometimes it is possible to get three crops a year, an enormous yield. But that also means that wild flowers and herbs get cut before they have a chance to flower and propagate.

The old way was to graze the fields over winter, then, somewhere at the beginning of April, take out the cattle and let the grass grow. In the higher dales haymaking was sometimes delayed, for weather and other reasons, until the middle of July or even towards the end of August.

I understand that Miss Hauxwell usually didn't cut her grass until well into August, so that gave the plants plenty of time to bloom and seed. And there was only one cut a year. The old way of farming.

So that was what I was doing in Baldersdale – looking for survivors in what has long been known to be a botanically rich area. One glance at Hannah's meadows told me that it had very real prospects because it did not have the lush, emerald green appearance of chemically fertilized land. It was a thin, washed out, yellowy green – just the kind of grass to excite a botanist. And it certainly turned out to be of considerable scientific interest.

There were dozens of species, including lady's mantle which has a very delicate green-and-yellow flower, and in certain varieties grows nowhere else in Britain. Another rare one was adder's tongue, a fern growing four inches above the ground with rather fleshy, pale green, diamond-shaped leaves. From the base of the leaf a spike appears, bearing two lots of bobbles containing thousands of fern spores. But the percentage of germination is very low, which was another reason for its poor survival prospects. An even rarer plant doing nicely on Hannah's land was a relative of the adder's tongue, the moonwort, which has a similar structure, but is a bit more complicated. I have no idea why it has come to bear that name.

Then there was the frog orchid which was not a rare plant until its kind of habitat became rare, and the eyebright, a pale little semiparasitical flower which twines into the roots of grasses to take nourishment. It has a whole range of colours, from all white, to white with blue, purple or mauve spots.

The cuckoo flower was there too, a lovely pale pink or pastel mauve which was one of the commonest wild flowers in Britain fifty years ago, but in another fifty years may be difficult to find. And what I thought was the prettiest sight in Hannah's meadows was the *Geranium sylvaticum*, or hay sward, which is a beautiful blue with a tinge of violet. When it's growing wild and bold, these flowers give a spangled mauve colour to a field.

Yellow is also a dominant colour in Hannah's meadows, but closer examination reveals the bright blue of the harebell, the crimson of the ragged robin and many other delicate shades.

Altogether, Hannah's meadows constitute a very rare and beautiful piece of land which will now, thankfully, be preserved for ever and farmed always in the Hauxwell manner.

The complete list of plants and grasses surviving on Hannah's land reads like a poem. They include meadow foxdale, downy oatgrass, crested dog's-tail, wood horse-tail, red fescue, sweet vernal grass, wood anemone, bugle, wood crane's-bill, globeflower, floating sweetgrass and sharp-flowered rush.

The Durham Wildlife Trust has set up permanent areas for study, and a completely detailed survey of the flora and fauna has been started. Although the special nature of the flora has been established, little is known yet of the fauna and it is considered that the insect and invertebrate community will be equally fascinating.

9

Cotherstone's Hidden
Gastronomic Tradition – and
the Salty Secret of
Mrs Birkett's Success

The village of Cotherstone, situated four miles northwest of the market town of Barnard Castle, was an early target of the fledgeling tourist industry, since it was within easy charabanc reach of the conurbation of Darlington, Durham and even Newcastle upon Tyne. Day-trippers and weekend visitors have filled the streets and riverside paths every summer for more than sixty years, but only a tiny percentage are aware of the village's remarkable gastronomic distinction, about which most communities would continually drum up a publicity fanfare.

Cotherstone cheese has been discreetly celebrated for well over a century. *White's Directory* of 1840 ends its brief thirteen-line description by declaring: 'Cotherston [sic] is noted for the manufacture of cheese of the same form and quality as Stilton cheese'.

To be bracketed with Stilton, the very king of English cheeses, is praise indeed. And Cotherstone cheese is made to this day, as keen readers of the *Good Food Guide* will confirm, and is available for sale at Cotherstone's post office. Superb it is too, with a long list of discerning enthusiasts ordering it regularly. It is featured proudly on the cheeseboards of several temples of gastronomy, and richly deserves much wider acclaim.

There is a simple reason for its relative anonymity. As far as can be ascertained, the future of Cotherstone cheese appears to be in the hands of one lady. And she refuses absolutely to communicate with the media. Many feature and food writers from various newspapers and magazines have tried over the years to obtain information and interviews and all have been denied. Her identity is widely known in the village, but her wishes are respected and her name will not be revealed here. She is the last of a long line of illustrious cheesemakers and her regular clients can only hope that she will pass on her expertise to the next generation.

Hannah knows her, of course, but she is as tight-lipped about names and places as everyone else in Cotherstone.

A little bit of secrecy does no harm now, does it? The existence of Cotherstone cheese is not widely known but that is the way the lady wants it, and those who like it can always find it.

Mother used to make cheese when she was young and she said there was an awful lot of work attached to it. We had a cheese press at Low Birk Hatt but I never recall it being used by our family. It stood outside in the garden for years until John and Vera Brittain took over from the Thwaites at High Birk Hatt. They came the year after the big storm in 1947 and she decided she would turn their spare milk into cheese. I don't think she had any experience but she became friendly with Eleanor Fawcett who had, and Vera borrowed our cheese press. She obviously learned quickly because she began to sell it quite successfully.

Vera would supply us with some from time to time and I know Uncle was partial to it. But I have never been a lover of cheese myself, except with Christmas cake.

There were several known cheesemakers in Cotherstone and the best known was a former Miss Chipchase, who married into the Birkett family at West Park Farm, which is situated along the top road into Baldersdale. I do believe people came from far away to buy her cheeses.

The sole surviving member of that family still lives in Cotherstone, just a few yards down the road from Hannah's cottage. Mrs Margaret Nixon was born in 1920, the youngest child of Mrs Katharine Birkett, undoubtedly Cotherstone's most famous cheesemaker. She was celebrated in the media, was featured in a 1940s radio programme and built up an impressive list of clients. Sacheverell Sitwell, the Marchioness of Bristol and the Countess of Rosebery, plus a clutch of other aristocrats placed regular orders, and a certain Mrs Demarest of the Manor House, Harrold, Bedfordshire, used to send twelve small cheeses in lieu of Christmas cards to a selection of her titled friends. The price varied from one shilling (five new pence) to one shilling and sixpence a pound, postage extra! Mrs Nixon still cherishes letters of appreciation from eminent people.

Mother's success was due in some part to her brother, my uncle, Charles Chipchase, who went to London in the 1920s and got into conversation with a newspaper reporter. He wrote an article and everyone started asking for our cheeses.

Mother was born into a Quaker family living at Lathbury, a hamlet near Cotherstone, went to a Society of Friends boarding school and later attended a course on dairy work run

Mrs Birkett, the famous cheesemaker of Cotherstone, busy at work with her daughters (Beamish, North of England Open Air Museum)

by the North Riding County Council at Helmsley. She used to visit local farms, struck up a friendship with my Aunt Hannah and was introduced to Father. They married in 1910 and she came to live at West Park, where Father was farming with his sister, Hannah.

There were quite a few noted cheesemakers in Cotherstone at the time, including the Misses Hutchinson and the Hodgson family, and Aunt Hannah also used to make cheeses with the help of my Aunt Mary, who lived in Lartington, and showed them at Eggleston Show.

It's generally accepted that the herbiage of this area produces the milk necessary to make a fine cheese. The richness and variety of plant life in Teesdale is well known, particularly in the lower-lying areas where some plants common in the south have their northernmost limit. That, together with certain northern species, and the legacy of limestone soil created in the ice age makes for our lush meadowland.

Naturally, Mother began to put into practice what she had learned at Helmsley. But she used a different technique to the others when it came to the salting. The really busy time was in the spring after the cows had calved and there was plenty of milk. The morning's milk was poured, still warm, into a large pan and set by the fire because the temperature had to be kept around 93°. We used a floating thermometer. Rennet – a piece of calf's innards usually – was added straight away. No other starter was used. You had to keep stirring all the time and, after an hour or so, the milk set solid and then was gently cut to allow the whey to flow out, leaving the curd. It was quite pleasant to eat at this stage – the curds and whey of the Little Miss Muffet nursery rhyme. The curd was then put into a straining cloth and left to drip with a blanket wrapped round it to keep it warm. At this stage, most of the cheesemakers – all the others perhaps – placed the curd into a vat of brine. But mother crumbled it up and sprinkled dry salt over it instead.

Then it was packed into various sizes of moulds from pint pots for quick unmatured sale, to the larger, more standard shapes and pressed with huge stone weights for twenty-four hours. Each cheese was wrapped in muslin bandages, placed

Mrs Birkett, straining the fresh, warm milk (1938/9)

opposite, *Breaking up the curd*

in a warm drying room and turned and rewrapped regularly.

Different grass at various times of the year used to produce different cheese. June milk was the best and strongest because you could leave it to turn blue for Christmas. We used to charge the top price for that – one shilling and sixpence a pound. A lot of our well-to-do customers liked it blue. I suppose it made a change from Stilton. I still have a letter dated September 1939, just after the outbreak of war, saying that 'Sir Fowler Harrison would be obliged if Mrs Birkett would supply eight or nine pounds of Cotherstone cheese, going blue if possible, and another ready for eating at once'.

left, *Putting the curd into the vats*; right, *Pressing the curd*

Later on you got what we call the fog cheese, from the second crop of grass in the autumn after haymaking, which was very rich but did not rise quite as well. And, do you know, before the war we could turn the cows out in the lane outside the farm before breakfast on summer mornings to graze the hedgerows because there was just no traffic at that time.

Weighing the finished cheeses

We delivered it locally from a pony and trap and I don't suppose we made all that much until they wrote about Mother in the London newspaper. Then everybody wanted it and she had to give up a bit of buttermaking she also did to cope with the demand. Some people used to call and insist on taking one away before she was really ready to sell it. Local shops even sold postcards of a photograph of our farm.

She also found the time to raise five children – Tommy, Bill, Jack, Molly and myself, the youngest. We all had to help in the dairy. My father died in 1927, when I was seven, but Mother carried on making cheese until around 1940. She died in 1952 and I am now the only one of the family left alive.

Delivery day – Willy and Molly Birkett

No one carried on the cheesemaking tradition in our family, although West Park Farm is still owned by the Birketts, run as a beef farm by my sister-in-law and her young son.

So these days I have to buy my cheese like everyone else. I have tried the Cotherstone cheese made today but I prefer something a little drier. So I get Wensleydale for myself and Cheddar for my husband.

106

10

Dogs, Country Remedies ...and the Cow with a Left Hook

Since Hannah lived in total isolation for more than twenty-five years, never married or even formed a relationship with a man, it is not surprising that most of the care and affection she had to offer was lavished on animals. She loved them all, each and every species to be found in the average Baldersdale farmyard, but was devoted particularly to dogs and cows. Suppressed maternalism it may be, but her passion shines through and she can recall in detail some animals, particularly dogs, that have been dead for half a century and some that didn't even belong to her. A fondness for dumb beasts may have been in the Hauxwell blood, because her Uncle Tommy, not a sentimental man in his later years, was a compassionate 'amateur' vet in Baldersdale. A good working dog – at least one – is essential for any stock farmer but the Hauxwells didn't always have much luck in finding the right one.

The first dog I recall from my childhood was little Meg. We got her from Sidney Fawcett, but she had a rather unfortunate weakness. She just could not resist rabbits. Now that's a real nuisance with a working dog because it doesn't matter where you have your beasts gathered or which direction you want to drive your sheep, a rabbit is always likely to pop up and Meg would be off like a shot. So Uncle arranged an exchange with our relatives at Piercebridge, and we got an Old English sheepdog, black all over, and called Roy. He was a lovely dog, but no good at working.

The next really special one was Peter. I had left school by then, and I was allowed to choose him myself from a litter. I called him Peter, after his father, who used to tour around a bit and always came to see me when he was on his travels. He was black with a smooth coat, and not a bad working dog. Uncle had a bitch called Jill at the time and they had puppies which we gave to the neighbours. Jill would work for me if

Uncle wasn't around but as soon as he appeared she didn't care a fig for me and would be off to see what he wanted to do.

But Peter was mine, and we had some grand times together, throwing sticks down by the reservoir. There were other dogs down the years, but the time came when I was on my own, and got a bit low financially, so I was not able to afford one. When your income is not much above five or six pounds a week, as it was for me in the seventies, even a tin of dog food is out of the question.

But one day, after that first programme, some friends from Halifax arrived with a little black and white Border collie pup, so small he could only just manage to get over the doorstep. He was called Chip and he stayed with me for around eight years. Now I have neither the patience nor the ability to train and discipline a dog, and Chip could be a bit wayward and excitable, but he was sometimes quite useful if you wanted to set cattle away across the field.

He had probably the nicest nature of any dog I ever owned, and possessed the loveliest eyes, brown in colour, and he was my dog definitely. When other people made a fuss of him, he hardly bothered with them, preferring to go over to wherever I might be and just sit there looking at me with those eyes.

Chip slept in a chair in the kitchen and was always at the door to greet me when I got up in the morning. If he wasn't waiting for me, I would know that something was wrong. You see, unfortunately, he didn't have a strong physique and eventually started to take fits. I had Mr Harris, the vet, out to him once or twice, and he gave him tablets which worked miracles for a time. But then he went into a bad fit and didn't come out of it.

I was so desolate about Chip. It's such a want when they have been there so long, that it's like losing a human being.

I should never have had the next one but I was in need of something. A rough-coated collie called Tip, he was offered to me by some relatives down the dale whilst I still had Chip. I refused him then but I weakened when they asked again after Chip had gone. Tip was a bonny dog, but a bully – even with me to begin with – and a real problem when the walkers came

Hannah with Chip

through my land along the Pennine Way. He would chase after them with me in hot pursuit, so he had to go back. Tip just wasn't my kind of dog at all.

In years gone by there had been some clever dogs in Baldersdale. The Fawcetts had one very intelligent sheepdog called Park, and the Sayers had one called Darkie, who had an unfortunate habit of being run over by farm vehicles. Then there was Rover of Clove Lodge, a large black dog who wasn't exactly a friendly animal.

I had another upset after the unfortunate experience with Chip and Tip. A dear friend of mine from Middlesbrough brought me a dog which turned out to have distemper, and he died. But then the same lady found Tim for me. He used to live in Thirsk but his mistress became too ill to look after him. He was almost two years old when he came to me.

I must confess I was a little disappointed when I first saw him, because he looked such a little old scrap after me being used to sheepdogs. But what I really liked was his face and we have been together for around five years.

He is very affectionate, and I wouldn't be without him now, and he has been to the vet's for his injections so as to avoid another disaster. A veterinary is what Uncle Tommy might have been if there had been the money to send him away to train, because he was very good with animals. People in Baldersdale often used to come for him to help calve their cows and, on one occasion, he worked alongside our local vet at that time, Mr Joe Cosgrove, who said afterwards he was pretty good. And professional people don't usually throw compliments around like that. Uncle once set the leg of a bull in Sleetburn, which must have been a tricky job, and I well remember the occasion when one of our cows had a really bad calving and Uncle saw her through. He had rheumatism and was known to be a bit quick-tempered and impatient, but even Mother remarked how surprised she was at his skill and patience when it came to doctoring animals.

There was another man, across the dale, called Ralph Tarn, who was also handy as an amateur vet. Of course, people would do as much as they could on their own, partly because

Hannah with Tim

it wasn't easy to send for a vet in a faraway place like Baldersdale, which didn't have many telephones, and partly because of the expense.

It was much the same when it came to doctors for the people. There were one or two ladies in Baldersdale who were very good at midwifery, which was just as well when a baby was on the way and the doctor couldn't get there in time, or the weather impeded him. And we had several of the old remedies at Low Birk Hatt, such as wintergreen and knitbone, and particularly aconite. Both Mother and Uncle were great believers in aconite, for either man or beast. It's a clear, almost colourless liquid in a little bottle with a spout on it, and Mother would put on her glasses and measure a drop or two very carefully into a drink for us, or into the water for the cattle. If you had a cold, aconite would stop it from developing, or keep a bad cold from becoming something worse.

Sheep we usually treated ourselves. I might still have the odd tin of some oval golden tablets, big as gooseberries, which we used to give them for worms. And on the occasions when there was an epidemic of sheep scab we all went to the sheep-dipping tub kept by the Fawcetts, and later the Thwaites at High Birk Hatt, to double dip them in a special drench. I didn't like that much because it was so smelly, but a necessary evil.

I was very fond of the sheep, especially when there were lambs, as well as the pigs and hens, but the dogs and the cows were very dear to me. When I was left on my own after the death of Uncle, my beasts became my family, I suppose. I couldn't let Rosa go when the time came to sell up. I know she is old and won't last forever, but she has been a good and loyal friend to me and I will stand by her.

A lot of people still remember Her Ladyship, the little white cow which was featured such a lot in *Too Long a Winter*, and so do I, of course. It was a very sad day when she became too old, ill and weak to carry on, but Rosa replaced her in my affections.

Her Ladyship was a mistake really. Her mother was much too young to have a calf but the gate got left open, or maybe the bull knocked it down, and she was conceived.

When I bought her as a young heifer, a friend went on and on about how small she was until I wondered if I was going to have a beast left at all by the time she had finished. But she turned out to be a grand cow, and a good mother to lots of calves. There were several bulls in the dale, but I cannot recall any serious incidents with them, although I know they can be very dangerous. We had one called Stumpy, a Dales short-horn, light roan in colour, which we reared from a calf. He had a nice temperament and you could go up to him and stroke him without fear. We had another one I really liked who shouldn't really have been passed by the Ministry man because his horns were too long. Nowadays, I believe all bulls have to be dehorned.

You couldn't keep bulls for long or the strain in your herd would have been weakened by in-breeding, so there was a regular turnover, and quite often farms would loan out their bulls around the Dales before selling them out of the area.

As a matter of fact, the animal that caused the most trouble – and some pain for me – was a little black heifer, a Galloway and shorthorn cross. All was well at first, but when she calved it was another story. She had a grand lot of milk, but she wouldn't let me milk her. The only way to succeed occasion-ally was to try when her calf was suckling her.

I had some real performances with that cow. She had a special, very unusual way of kicking. She could bring her milking-side foot round in a curve and very fast. It was a sort of left hook.

She caught me a couple of times, did that beastie. I called her Blackie – and a good few more things as well, I can tell you!

Sheep dipping with the Thwaites family of High Birk Hatt, c. 1930

11

Hannah's Successors: the New Owners of Low Birk Hatt

T he question of who would succeed Hannah Hauxwell at Low Birk Hatt aroused keen interest both locally and nationally. Hannah decided to divide her property, which spread over 78 acres of unforgiving land, into three parcels and invite sealed bids.

The house, together with 15 acres, was one of the parcels.

It was thought likely that some substantial Teesdale farmer might buy all three, ranch the land and sell off the house as a weekend cottage – a regrettably common practice which has been partially responsible for the steady depopulation of the Dales, particularly the more isolated places.

Many other permutations were possible but the future of the house did cause worry. There was even a rumour that the local authority was to acquire it and turn it into some kind of museum.

The hope was that whoever followed Hannah would respect the character of Low Birk Hatt and, to some extent, carry on the way of life of the Hauxwells and their kin, the only family to have previously lived there.

The outcome was – eventually – to be deeply satisfying to everyone who cherishes the ecology and traditions of this wild and beautiful place.

To begin with, the main pastures were bought by the Durham Wildlife Trust (see Chapter 8) and will be protected for all time. It has to be said that the prospects for the house and farm buildings did not seem promising when Gordon Pratt of Hawes Auction Mart opened the bids on 28 October 1988. The successful one was made by a couple totally unknown in Teesdale. Nor were they farmers. And total anonymity was demanded, so the waiting Press and television crews went away empty-handed.

They still want their identities to remain publicly un-announced. Their names and background are known to their neighbours in Baldersdale but they are very anxious to avoid as much as possible becoming involved in the publicity which continually surrounds Hannah and hope that interest in her former home will eventually decline and disappear. However, they have agreed to reveal their detailed plans for Low Birk Hatt and they are calculated to please the most critical defender of Dales traditions.

He is a successful business executive with all the trappings – heavy responsibilities, large car, mobile phone – and she also has a career, with professional qualifications. But both have their roots in the land and within a reasonably short space of time Low Birk Hatt is due to emerge, its amenities vastly improved, as a family home with cattle grazing the land around it.

Just as it always has been.

And he is quick to point out that it was a joint decision to make a serious bid.

Yes, we had both been searching for years for a place like this, well away from urban life with some land and outbuildings. We live about an hour's drive away from Baldersdale and every weekend we would scour the 'Property for Sale' columns of the local newspapers. When we saw Low Birk Hatt advertised in the *Darlington and Stockton Times*, we realized who it belonged to because we had seen the television programmes.

We did wonder if we would manage to find the place but we located it one wet Sunday afternoon. As we walked through the gate, Hannah popped out of the byre and asked us to wait until she had finished showing someone else round. Then she shut us in the byre – and we stayed there a long time!

She was most meticulous in her guided tour, opening every door. And as we drove away, we hadn't travelled down the road very far when my wife looked at me in a certain way . . . and I knew that she wanted Low Birk Hatt as much as me.

It is going to be a family home. We have two sons, one already away pursuing a career and the other about to take A levels. So we won't be tied down to schools very much longer. And I have a job which involves quite a lot of travel so I am not too restricted about where I live. Incidentally, both boys are enthusiastic about the place.

Hannah and her 'family'

The new owner of Low Birk Hatt digging out for the new road

We have a two-year plan, which I hope will not turn into a rolling two years! Then we aim to sell our present home and move in permanently. It's proving to be a strain, both financially and physically – since we are doing as much of the work ourselves as possible – and our friends were convinced for some time that we had gone mad!

The first major thing I did was to have a road laid from the top, rather a long way. I dug out some of the wet land and a local man put down a crushed stone track in four days, so we can now drive from the main road almost to the front door. It was done with the co-operation and permission of the Nature Conservancy Council so as to avoid ecological damage, and I would like to point out politely that it is a private road.

A septic tank has already been installed and I have a quotation – amounting to some thousands of pounds, I'm

Finished – the road to Low Birk Hatt

afraid – to drill for water. But it has to be done. Judging from geological surveys, they expect to have to go down to a depth of 45 metres before they find it. And they won't give any guarantees, although I understand they haven't failed up to now.

We have bought an Aga, and intend to have central heating, probably oil-fired, as well as open fires. Inside, the walls have been damp-proofed by injection and I have re-layed the stone floor flags myself. In the big front room the flags were as good as new – no wear at all –. and Hannah told me it had only been used for funerals and pig-killings.

I knew that Hannah had experienced problems with rodents so I expected to find rat runs and nests underneath the flags, but only mice had been there. I have only seen two rats, and they were both outside the house and both dead. But I did discover where they had been coming in – through the stable

122

and into the wall – and where they had resided when I pulled down the ceiling lathes in the dairy and a load of old nests and rat droppings fell on to my head.

The only wildlife problem has been created by the jackdaws trying to nest in the front-room chimney, so I have pushed up a chimney brush to discourage them. That chimney turned out to be the only delicate part of the building and scaffolding had to be erected so that it could be rebuilt. Of course, that job had to be done professionally – by a local man, because I am trying to use local contractors wherever possible.

A farmer friend of mine came to look the place over shortly after we bought it and he gave me some useful advice: that, whatever happened, we must enjoy doing the work. I tried to keep his words in the front of my mind, particularly during the bad times when we were clearing everything out and the dust and debris of a hundred years was falling into our eyes. But, now we are beginning to put things back, I am feeling a sense of achievement.

The outbuildings, like the byre and the barn, will have to wait until later. The roof of the barn concerns me because eventually it will fall in but I dare not start on it just yet – the house must take priority.

Some of our precious time spent at Low Birk Hatt is taken up by a steady stream of Hannah's admirers, making a pilgrimage to a place they know so well from the television programmes and books. Most of them are very courteous and we haven't minded them having a quick look round, but some are less welcome. I hope this public interest will eventually fade away, especially when we have moved in for good.

When we do so, I intend to carry on with my job, which has agricultural connections. My original career intention was to go into farm management and I went to agricultural college. I worked on farms for a while before I joined my present company, so I know how to handle a tractor!

His wife has even closer links with farming. She is the daughter of an arable farmer situated well south of Teesdale, in an area where both she and her husband were born and brought up. And,

Converting the stable at Low Birk Hatt

Rebuilding the 'delicate' chimney

remarkably, she has formed an affectionate bond with Rosa, Hannah's much loved senior cow, which for part of the year returns to her old pastures because Bill Purves, the neighbour who cares for Rosa, rents the grazing from the new owners.

Rosa really is an old dear. She comes up to the house and starts bellowing, and just will not stop until you give her a cuddle! I intend to keep cows when we move in, very much the same way as Hannah.

We both know about farming – we even met at a Young Farmers' dance! And the isolation at Low Birk Hatt will not worry me, even when my husband is away on business, because my father's place was even lonelier.

The prospect of winters here is something we will have to prepare for carefully. A four-wheel-drive vehicle will be an essential, of course, and my husband can leave his car at the top on the main road when snow is forecast.

The commitment which the new proprietors are bringing to the enormous task of totally renovating and modernizing Low Birk Hatt is patently obvious. For years they have denied themselves many of the luxuries they would otherwise have been easily able to afford because they both knew that one day they would need the capital to spend on the kind of home they both dreamed about. She even volunteered to do without an engagement ring, a classic case of long-term planning, if ever there was one.

Most weekends, they labour side by side to conserve funds for the jobs they cannot tackle. Their summer holidays are spent in the caravan they have positioned in the yard.

They have won the respect of their neighbours in Baldersdale, and even Hannah, although still psychologically adjusting herself to Low Birk Hatt belonging to someone else, is aware that her old family home is in good hands.

I liked them very much as soon as I met them, that very damp Sunday afternoon. And they were so patient as they waited for me to finish with my other visitors. I took them into the byre so that they could shelter from the rain.

Hannah with the new mistress of Low Birk Hatt

They were among a few people who came back to see over the property again quite a few times, and I met their sons. I talked to the lady for some time and we seemed to like the same things, so I was pleased when their bid was the successful one.

I did wonder at first whether or not they realized what they were taking on because Baldersdale is another world compared to what they have been accustomed to – very different indeed.

But it is good to know they have experience of farming and intend to make it a proper home and keep cattle. And I am very pleased she is kind to my poor Rosa – very pleased indeed.

When I handed over I did offer to come back and help, do a bit of walling for them, perhaps, but I didn't know then just how busy my life would be when I came to Cotherstone. I imagined I would have a lot of spare time, but my diary is always full.

Nor did I realize how difficult it would be to face up to going back. I'm frightened now that it will unsettle me, bring back too many memories.

But I am happy for them to be there and wish them well.

12

Meeting the Public...
the Wogan Shows...
and What the Papers Say

One of the many unusual facets of Hannah Hauxwell is her reaction to certain situations which would daunt much more apparently sophisticated people and which one would expect to be overwhelming for a simple soul from the back of beyond, such as meeting, on level terms, some of the famous and mighty, or appearing in front of milling crowds, and even standing up to address them.

But Miss Hannah Hauxwell is neither daunted nor overwhelmed. Whatever the grandeur of the situation, she transcends it with a sweet serenity which mesmerizes everyone. There have been many classic occasions down the years, one as far back as 1973 when the writer of this piece was a makeweight speaker at a *Yorkshire Post* literary lunch in Harrogate, attended by four hundred elegant people – mostly well-heeled, middle-aged ladies in all their finery. The heavily publicized leading speaker was an exceedingly famous television personality of the day, who shall remain nameless. Now, whenever this writer mentioned the name of Hannah Hauxwell, who was seated alongside him, he noticed a distinct ripple of excitement in the audience. So, as he concluded, he asked Hannah to stand up and just say 'hello' – that's all. To everyone's astonishment, she addressed the gathering with style and modest confidence for several minutes. The place exploded.

For the next two hours the literary lunchers surged around Hannah and virtually ignored the ostensible star of the show, who had been obliged to immediately follow Hannah and had fallen flat. He was not pleased.

Hannah never appears to be overawed by the great names. Whether it is royalty, legendary sportsmen or major politicians and broadcasters, she meets them all with much aplomb. More often than not, they turn out to be admirers, well versed in her background, and she finds herself answering the sort of urgent

128

questions that 'normal people' ask when they are introduced to her: how is she settling to her new life?; does she miss Low Birk Hatt and her beasts?; is she taking care of herself?; and so on.

These days Hannah keeps an engagement diary. She is in constant demand to make public appearances and to give television and other media interviews. To accept them all would place an intolerable strain on her health, but she rarely fails to help a charity. She firmly refuses to concede that she is a celebrity, merely saying that she 'leads two lives' but is essentially an ordinary Daleswoman. But the effect she has whenever she does meet her devotees is startling. She has been known to stop the traffic on one of her book-signing sessions, a situation which eventually required the police to gently and good-humouredly sort it out. She has created records at most of the bookshops she has attended. On one December Saturday, Hannah sat in the Craven Herald Bookshop in Skipton and people queued through the premises, out of the door, down an alleyway and along the High Street. At any one time there were three hundred people patiently waiting in the most appalling weather. Many were there for more than three hours, but Hannah always gives full value for this kind of sacrifice, talking to each one for between five and fifteen minutes and writing in the book whatever message is asked for. There was a great deal of camaraderie in evidence and several promising friendships were forged in the crowd. Bookshop staff went round handing out sweets and, as the light faded, a portable telephone was taken along the line for those who wanted to tell their friends and relatives why they would be so late home. One woman walked for an hour through the snow to catch the bus to Skipton, waited for three and a half hours to meet Hannah, and still went home smiling.

Along with the hundred copies Hannah dealt with the following day for those who had been unable to reach Skipton, the staggering figure of five hundred books were signed. Many thousands more have been sold at bookshop appearances from the northeast to the Midlands, whilst at the Grove Bookshop in Ilkley, run by Andrew Sharp, *Seasons of My Life – the Story of a*

Book-signing session – a chat with an admirer

Solitary Daleswoman, is, by a huge margin, the most popular book ever stocked.

Television stations from Tyne Tees in the northeast, via Yorkshire Television (of course) in Leeds (the *Calendar* programme named Hannah 'Woman of the Decade') to TV-AM in London regularly ask her to appear in their studios, and often send film crews to Cotherstone. Without exception, the programme-makers depart gleefully with the material. Hannah always delivers – she is a natural communicator. Placing a camera in any situation usually diminishes it in some way, but the opposite is true of Hannah – the camera adores her.

Travelling the celebrity circuit has led to some fascinating encounters with certain household names including two sessions with the top talk-show man of his time, Terry Wogan.

Now, I must confess I hadn't seen much of Mr Wogan before I met him because, when I got my television set at Low Birk

Hatt, Richard Megstone, the nice young gentleman who looked after the Youth Hostel in Baldersdale and kindly took care of my electrical things, said I had a choice – either BBC1 or Channel 4. And I chose Channel 4. I recall hearing Mr Wogan on the wireless, but he was basically a stranger to me. So I went with an open mind.

I always enjoy going to London. It is our capital city, after all, and it is quite exciting to see the sights and stay in those lovely hotels – I like travelling by train too. Kathy Rooney, who worked with Barry Cockcroft for many years at Yorkshire Television, escorted me down on both occasions. This time in the hotels I particularly noticed how many people of different tongues were also staying there – all babbling away and making me wonder who they were and where they had come from. Quite fascinating! Some of the staff hailed from foreign parts too. I've had some interesting conversations with several of them, talking about opera with an Italian waiter, for instance. On another occasion, a lovely lady called Elsa who came to tidy my room, and who was from a South American country, took me into her confidence and told me about some of the problems she was facing. Quite a sad story really. And a gentleman who I think was Chinese had an accident with some plates whilst serving a meal, and finished up by giving me a kiss!

But those hotels are so big and confusing. I'm no good at getting into lifts and finding my room so someone always has to show me. The Kensington Hilton was enormous, quite the biggest place I have ever encountered to date. A person like me can easily get lost there – and I did! Kathy Rooney had to leave me one night when we were dining at the Kensington Hilton, so she took me to the porter to arrange for him to take me upstairs to my room when I was ready. But when I later tried to find my way back to the dining-room to finish my meal, which should have been a simple thing to do, I just could not locate it at all. Eventually I stopped a very helpful young lady member of the staff, told her of my predicament and she guided me back to my table.

I was very nervous when I went to meet Mr Wogan for the

first time but the gentleman who drove the big car to the show was very nice and friendly. He took me to the BBC Studios in Shepherd's Bush and I was introduced to the lady producer, who was charming. We stood a good few minutes in the entrance hall, and a gentleman came through and smiled, and someone said it was Billy Graham, Mr Wogan's other guest. But I wouldn't have recognized him. Then we went upstairs to the make-up room and Mr Wogan came to say a quick hello, which is his custom, I believe. But I wasn't there at the time. We did meet briefly in the doorway and I think he said something. I was a bit flustered at the time so I don't really know what he said.

I was given the opportunity to have a rehearsal with him but I declined because I am not like the professionals who can rehearse in detail and then put it over as fresh as a daisy when the time comes. So the first time I had a conversation with Mr Wogan was live on television!

Mind, I did rehearse the walk-on, which is quite critical. Kathy Rooney stood in for Mr Wogan, and I was a bit tense when it came to the real thing. But it seemed to go all right. I think they rather wanted me to wear my old farm clothes, but we compromised with a grey check skirt which a good friend gave me, and a blue jumper. I had been in television studios before but never with a live audience, so that was a bit different. After I got started and into the conversation I felt a lot more comfortable. I enjoyed talking to him, and thought him a very good interviewer – and that makes all the difference. After the programme we exchanged a few words, but he had to dash off to another engagement. Dr Billy Graham was also busy, and we met briefly in the doorway. I seemed to meet everyone in doorways that evening. But the lady producer and her researcher, Cathy Meade, were both very complimentary about me.

In fact they were clearly entranced by Hannah – which, it has to be said, is par for the course with everyone meeting this lady for the first time. Terry Wogan became so absorbed with her that he ran the interview into the closing music, leaving him scant time to promote his next programme – very unusual. The audience response was equally enthusiastic and Hannah was urgently requested to return to take part in *The Wogan Christmas Show*.

Oddly enough, I didn't happen to be in my room again when Terry Wogan came to see me before the show on the second occasion. Poor man – I don't know what he thought about me, but that's just the way it happened. And this time I didn't have to walk on because I was already installed on the sofa when the show began. Nor did we have a talk beforehand because he was on the stage doing a turn with somebody else – I think they call it a warm-up. There was an embarrassing moment when I thought he was walking over to me to begin the programme and I got up to greet him. But he called out, 'No, sit down, Hannah, sit down, we are not starting yet!'

That unsettled me a bit, but we eventually got going and it was all right. I have to say I enjoyed the first programme much more, simply because of the subject we had to discuss on the second one, which was Christmas. You see, I don't like Christmas very much because it brings back all those painful memories of the years when I was on my own and there wasn't much money – not much of anything at all. It is something inside me. I've had good Christmases since but it's a feeling I cannot shed. It's something, as I said on the programme, that I cannot be all starry-eyed and bushy-tailed about. So I was quite happy to sit back and let the other guests talk when they came on.

Afterwards, there was a little Christmas party in the entertainment room upstairs, and all the Wogan studio team came. Mr Wogan arrived and had a few words with me – and everybody else – but once again I don't recall what we talked about. The trouble is, I get all of a whirl at times like that. Mrs Wogan was there too. She was very nice and we exchanged a few pleasant words. Such a charming lady.

The Press has been conducting a romance with Hannah for nearly two decades. Reporters and feature writers wore a path through the pastures of Low Birk Hatt, and now they knock constantly on the door of Belle Vue Cottage, Cotherstone. Many miles of film have been exposed and several forests felled to supply the paper to print the wit and wisdom of Hannah Hauxwell. The British Press habitually looks for an opportunity eventually to knock down the heroes they have created and placed on pedestals, if only to do something new. Some writers probably set off with that idea in the back of their minds, but up to now Hannah has disarmed them all.

A perfect example of how Hannah emerges unscathed from the most penetrating analysis is contained in Alan Frank's well-constructed piece in *The Times* of January 1990. It begins:

'If you had not been told otherwise, you might think it was all a terrific affectation – this old woman from the Dales with the luminescent skin, the saintly set of the features and the clothes from the pile which even the rag-and-bone man would probably not take. . . . She has become what might be called The Professional Daleswoman.

It is enough to make you smell a rat and be damned for your cynicism.

Hannah Hauxwell is famous for being obscure, which by definition is a state of affairs that cannot last. She is one of those official curios so beloved by the British in their presentation of the living heritage – a Listed Person, withstanding the erosions of the impure present.

Yet if this extraordinary ordinary woman does get a private frisson of vanity from her fame then hers is a classy act of concealment. "I'm not a celebrity," she says with a levelness I was told to expect. "My assessment of myself is that I am a plain Daleswoman . . ." '

In the *Observer*, Janet Watts had no reservations: 'Hannah received me with the warmth and courtesy she radiates in the film and talked for three hours without any refreshment but a tooth-glass of tap water, in which she toasted my health.'

Byron Rogers, writing eloquently in the *Sunday Express Magazine*, was most concerned about the confusion of possessions Hannah had crammed into her new home:

'I offered advice. The room we sat in contained two television sets, two oak sideboards, slightly lower than the ceiling and four clocks all stopped at different times. "Miss Hauxwell," I said, "you'll have to throw something away."

Miss Hannah Hauxwell, dressed in men's trousers and old jacket so torn that it looked as though savaging by wolf packs had once been part of her daily routine, looked at me mildly. "I am no admirer of President Reagan," she said in her precise way. "But I must quote him here: You ain't seen nothing yet."

There was a mangle in one room rearing up out of the cardboard boxes like a stag, the chaos (or the wolves) had not yet pulled down. But it was a neat chaos of boxes piled on each other, cakes still in the tins they came in and hatboxes, one of which contained the last remaining ball of her long-ago childhood. In the passage, done up with string and still unopened, were the parcels and Christmas cards sent by the world and his brother when they learned she was moving home three months ago. . . !

Byron Rogers ended his lavishly illustrated piece with the words: 'This has been a late twentieth-century fable'.

Nancy Banks-Smith of the *Guardian*, consistently one of the best writers in journalism today, first wrote stylishly about Hannah in 1973, and in her review of the last film declared:

' "A Winter Too Many" was the elegaic end of a besieged life . . . the enthralling thing about Hannah, when Barry Cockcroft made that first documentary, "Too Long A Winter", was not the things she managed without: warmth, water, company, money. The world, I am pleased to say, is full of unreasonable old women. The thing about Hannah is Hannah herself.

Her voice was soft and low; her complexion a child's. She was so transparent that there seemed nothing but clear skin between what she felt and what she said. Something shone through. The effect was nunlike even to the headscarf which she wore indoors and out, like a wimple. This kind of shine, you felt, must come from a renunciation, not necessarily religious, of the world . . .'

But Miss Banks-Smith went on to worry about the effects of such overwhelming attention: 'You wonder with something like guilt whether television was good for her'. It *was* good to her. Viewers, touched by her life, sent gifts of money which she used to buy not comforts for herself but more cows, and that meant more crippling winter work. Well-wishers exerted a steady, gentle, concerned pressure on her to be sensible.

Financially, she was now as they say, quite warm. This Wordsworthian woman was transformed into a nice old lady in a cottage with a window through which to watch, as she said, 'the world go by'.

Most newspapers have simply reflected the public adulation: 'Unique Figure Fascinates Eleventh Telegraph Literary Luncheon' was the nine-column headline in the *Grimsby Evening Telegraph*: 'She was its star . . . she captivated the 330-strong audience with her simple charm'. One of the 'important' speakers was Tony Benn!

Another banner headline in the *Evening Gazette*, Middlesbrough, resulted from a tumultuous signing session, at Dresser's Bookshop in Darlington: 'Hannah, Oh Hannah! Magnificent Daleswoman'. The *Teesdale Mercury* ran 'Hannah Is The Star Attraction', whilst the *Darlington and Stockton Times* declared, after one of Hannah's appearances, that she 'received the sort of welcome normally reserved for royalty'.

13

Olive Field: the Lady of Lartington Hall

*T*oo Long a Winter, the film documentary which projected Hannah Hauxwell into her stellar position in the affections of the British public (and far beyond) wasn't really about Hannah at all. It actually told the story of an entire Teesdale community of which Hannah was just one member, albeit a 'lead' in the dramatic sense. But the viewers were blinkered. For them, no one else in the programme existed – except one. And since that happened to be another woman, she had to be remarkable – and she certainly was. Olive Julia Field was the lady in the Big House, Lartington Hall, just down the road from Hannah's cottage in Cotherstone, and the owner of large tracts of land locally, including chunks of Baldersdale. A widow in her eighties, disabled and wheelchair-bound by arthritis, caused in the main by many hunting accidents, she held an annual Harvest Home in her private chapel, followed by feasting and dancing in the ballroom, to which she invited estate workers and local luminaries. Hannah went too, and the cameras followed. Mrs Field's forthright manner, allied to a distinct sense of humour and a stentorian voice, made a deep impression on the director and his crew – and on the television critics of the major newspapers, to judge by the reviews published the day after the first of many transmissions of *Too Long a Winter*. She was virtually the only 'survivor', in publicity terms, of the remainder of the film's cast.

In her review in the *Guardian*, Nancy Banks-Smith even gave equal space to Mrs Field after her eulogy of Hannah:

'At the other end of the social see-saw was Mrs Field of Lartington Hall, widow of the grandson of millionaire Marshall Field. She is equally her own person. An exuberant hostess and a handful even in her eighties.

' "I think it's about time we were going to chapel, Madam'', said her companion. "Oh, the hell'', replied Mrs Field.'

In the *Morning Star*, a newspaper not given to writing about the rich and over-privileged, Stewart Lane wrote:

'The closing part of the programme was quite unforgettable, with the local lady of the manor, Mrs Field, combining Harvest Festival with America's Thanksgiving.

I didn't actually see anyone touch their forelock, but from the moment when Mrs Field accompanied the entry of the turkey with blasts of a hunting horn, to shots of Hannah primly seated, timidly moving one foot to the music, I knew this was a world far removed, not only in distance but in time, from the pace of urban life in which I move.'

Olive Julia Field has been accurately described as a well-loved eccentric. She was certainly a true daughter of a remarkably colourful family, for she was born a Saunderson, a line of famous

Mrs Field demonstrates her technique with the hunting horn during the filming of Too Long a Winter *in 1972* (Courtesy of Yorkshire Television)

Protestant fighters who were sent to settle in Ireland in the seventeeth century to quell the local rebels. They were given a large slice of counties Cavan and Fermanagh, including 20,000 acres from a grateful Cromwell after Robert Saunderson led troops to a famous victory at Drogheda. The Saundersons endured a rough passage when Catholic James II decreed that Protestants be persecuted in their turn, and Robert, the son of Cromwell's favourite, had to flee with a price on his head.

The family clung on, and Olive's father, Llewellyn, was one of three Saunderson brothers who cut a dash in nineteenth-century Dublin society as officers in the Eleventh Hussars. In 1863, he fell in love with one of the most beautiful women of the viceregal court, Lady Rachael Scott, daughter of the Earl of Clonmell. But the Earl vehemently opposed the match and would not even allow Llewellyn to enter his house.

The stricken suitor followed the tradition laid down in these matters and went to look for a fight. He volunteered to join the Regiment of Irish Light Horse, raised to go to the assistance of the Confederate forces in the American Civil War. By the time the two sides prepared to meet on the field of Gettysburg, Llewellyn had risen to be the aide-de-camp to General Robert E. Lee, the Confederate commander. Llewellyn created another Saunderson legend in the midst of that bloody battle. He was unhorsed, helpless and about to perish as a Federal trooper rode at him, sword raised. Llewellyn was a quick thinker, and gave the Masonic sign of distress on the faint chance that the trooper was also a member of the order. It worked. The trooper returned the salute with his sword and rode on by. General Lee lost the battle and surrendered, and so yet another Saunderson was on the run. But Llewellyn, as resourceful as his ancestors, gave his pursuers the slip and managed to find his way to the port of New Orleans where he boarded a ship bound for Ireland.

Llewellyn's exploits became the talk of Dublin and the hostility of the Earl of Clonmell melted. He gave his consent to the marriage and Llewellyn and Rachael lived for twenty years in Drunkeen, one of the Saunderson family homes. Olive was born there and might have stayed in Ireland for good but for the civil unrest created by the Irish demands for home rule at the time. In

1886, Llewellyn and his family were hissed and booed when they went to church. In dramatic Saunderson fashion, Llewellyn declared he was finished with Ireland and left to spend his later years travelling Europe, the young and lovely Olive in tow. They wintered in San Moritz.

Olive Saunderson and Norman Field met and fell in love in predictably romantic circumstances, when the Fields and the Saundersons were guests on board Lord Vestey's yacht on a cruise to Norway in 1909. They were married the same year in Dublin and returned to England to set up home.

The family Olive Saunderson married into had a story to equal her own, also stretching back to the seventeenth century when Zachariah Field left Yorkshire to settle in Massachusetts as a yeoman farmer. Norman Field's father was born there in 1831. His brother, Marshall Field, arrived three years later and went on to become a world legend as the Merchant Prince.

At the age of twenty-one, after some years as a clerk in a dry-goods store, Marshall went to Chicago, telling his sceptical boss that he would one day own a store so big that the doors alone would be worth more than the boss's entire business. It proved to be a conservative estimate. Marshall Field, who arrived in Chicago with one dollar in his pocket, built one of the world's greatest department stores and had enough spare energy to partner Pullman in the railcar business, become vice-president of both General Electric and the Edison Company, president of United States Steel, founder of the *Chicago Sun* and a bank which became one of the four biggest in the world. And he still found time to build up vast interests in meat packing and combine-harvesting giants. Gordon Selfridge, who went on to do rather well himself in the department-store business, started as one of Marshall's clerks. He was fired for impertinence. Marshall Field died in 1905 at the age of seventy-one. Five thousand of his employees attended the funeral. He left a personal fortune of $120 million, a staggering sum when the mathematical equation to bring it into line with its value today is calculated.

Norman's father, Marshall Field's elder brother, Joseph, did rather well himself in banking before accepting a job with Marshall. In 1879 he was sent to England to oversee the

Olive Field in her VAD uniform, 1914

Norman Field, Master of Lartington Hall

European side of the business, and settled in Cheshire within easy reach of the textile mills of Lancashire where he placed a lot of business. He had men in Paris, Berlin, Rome, Belfast and elsewhere to search out the merchandise needed to satisfy the voracious appetite of the Chicago store and, by 1875, was dispatching three-million-dollars' worth of goods each year across the Atlantic.

Norman was born in Altrincham, Cheshire, in 1880. He went to Eton where he began a lifelong interest in hunting by becoming Master of the Beagles. After completing his education he went to work in the family's Chicago businesses, but the call of the land, which ran strongly in his blood, proved too much. He went farming in Texas, but returned to England in 1908 and bought Morris Grange, with four farms, at Scotch Corner – a few miles from Lartington.

Severance from the family business did not reduce Norman's standard of living. In 1924, for instance, his income from the Field Family Trust in the United States, after all taxes were met, was £42,000. That, with what would certainly be substantial assets and income from other sources, combined with whatever part of the Saunderson fortune was brought into the marriage by Olive, allowed the Fields to indulge in a stylish and lavish way of life.

It was a permanent party, with a little gentlemanly farming on the side – interrupted, it must be said, by two World Wars when both laboured mightily for the common cause. From Morris Grange they hunted assiduously – their joint passion since they never had children of their own.

Norman became joint Master of the Zetland and, in 1924, took over the Westmeath Hounds in Eire. Every winter season he and Olive would entrain for the Saundersons' homeland, together with a selection of staff (said to number over sixty at one stage) and horses. Knockrin Castle was rented from Lord Boyne and the revelry was ceaseless.

On one of their visits, there was an uncanny, if hilarious, echo of the kind of political and religious turmoil experienced by Olive's family in years gone by. One day they were boarding a boat and noticed it contained a large number of sticks, shaped like rifles. On enquiring their purpose, the boatman explained they were used for drilling by the Orangemen on the estate, but they were passed on each week to the Sinn Feiners for their drill night!

Both Olive and Norman were skilled riders. Norman became a four-handicap polo player. He was devoted to sport, golfing around the world's best courses and still finding time to be an active member of the Royal Yacht Squadron. He owned a 70-ton yacht called *Revive*.

Olive's surplus energy was spent in working for the Red Cross Society and forming a Girl Guide and Scout troop. When Norman went to serve with the East Riding Yeomanry during the First World War, reaching the rank of captain, she worked from 7.00 a.m. to 5.00 p.m. as a VAD at the Red Cross Hospital in Richmond, travelling each day by pony and trap or bicycle, carrying a fresh egg from one of the Field farms. Soused herring was the standard hospital breakfast and she declared she couldn't stomach that at seven o'clock in the morning. Days off were spent riding to hounds. Grand though she was, she was rarely allowed to do any nursing, beyond changing the odd dressing. So she spent most of her time scrubbing floors. When war came again in 1939, she turned part of Lartington Hall into a convalescent hospital for war-wounded. The ballroom became a dormitory and two thousand servicemen passed through. Olive, acting as unpaid commandant with her customary zeal, was made a life member of the Red Cross, a signal honour. For his part, Norman handed over his yacht to the Royal Navy.

But when the nation was not at war the social round of the Fields was formidable. Olive, it is said, eventually grew tired of Morris Grange so, in 1919, Norman bought Lartington Hall with its 140 acres of parkland, 2 grouse moors, 2 lakes, 12 farms and most of the cottages in the village, and it became their principal residence for the rest of their lives. At the same time he also acquired the Streatlam Castle estate, childhood home of the Queen Mother, from the Earl of Strathmore. Consideration was given to living there, but the thought of sixty bedrooms and only one bathroom was too much. Legend has it that the place was once so deprived of modern conveniences that drinking water would sometimes be collected by a footman with a silver pitcher from a stream flowing in front of the main door, which originally served as a moat.

They gave Morris Grange, as a present, to the Red Cross as a home for sick children from the Teesdale area and considered how to improve Streatlam. The castle was in such a state of disrepair that they decided not to spend money on it, and eventually it was demolished. They chose instead to spend large sums of money on the farms, rebuilt the famous Orangery and installed a large indoor swimming pool in the courtyard. Norman also established a breeding stud of racehorses which produced many classic winners. A crowded board recalling the names of the stud's successful horses, along with several equestrian paintings, graced the reception area of Lartington Hall. They now reside on the walls of Rules of Covent Garden, said to be London's oldest restaurant, which is run by the son of Mrs Fields' nephew, John Mayhew.

Naturally, one of the first things the Fields did on arrival at Lartington Hall was to start their own pack of hounds. They went hunting most days of the season. The Hunt Balls are still recalled today with something akin to awe in the villages of Lartington and Cotherstone where several former servants of the Fields live in retirement. Mrs Betty Pearson, the lady who sold Belle Vue Cottage to Hannah, was one. She walked into Cotherstone at seven o'clock every morning to keep house for the 'Bothy Boys', the lads who looked after the hounds. Her husband, Jack, used to sell fruit and vegetables from a horse and cart, going as far as the top of Baldersdale to find custom. He was well known to all the elder members of the Hauxwell family, including Hannah's mother and father.

One particular family in Cotherstone must be able to claim the longest aggregate of service to the Fields, amounting to some hundreds of years. Mrs Dorothy Siswick was Olive Field's last personal maid. Her father was Head Groomsman at Streatlam, her mother the cook and her brother a footman. Her husband, Harry, was the head gardener to Lartington. Mrs Siswick first met Mrs Field when she was living with her parents at one of the estate cottages at Streatlam.

It was in 1924 when I was fourteen that I first went to work for Mrs Field. She came to visit Streatlam to look at the horses and

Mr and Mrs Siswick in 1990 (Courtesy of *Teesdale Mercury*)

I thought what a very handsome woman she was. She looked me over, said I seemed to be a nice girl and announced that she had just the job for me – taking her goats out for a walk! I was paid a few pence, and very welcome it was too.

When I was eighteen she gave me the job of housekeeper in the big cottage she kept at Streatlam to entertain her friends coming to swim in the pool and play tennis. They arrived from all over the place, from the big houses locally to as far away as London. They certainly knew how to enjoy themselves in those days. I would get a phone call to say they were coming, and sometimes I had to cook lunch for as many as sixty people. Occasionally, after a dance, they would decide to go swimming in the early hours of the morning, so all the cars would be lined up with their headlamps blazing to light up the pool.

Mrs Field was such a grand lady, and eventually I moved to Lartington to become her lady's maid. She could be abrupt at times but never held a grudge, and Mr Field was a real gentleman, always kind and polite. He broke his hip whilst hunting and the poor man walked with a limp from then on. Mrs Field rode to hounds twice a week, and I had to prepare and lay out her clothes before and after the hunt. Quite often she would return in such a mess, all covered in mud. She had one or two accidents in the field herself, and once broke her arm. In later years she suffered very badly from arthritis.

Mr and Mrs Field had separate bedrooms, which was the habit of the gentry. Every night the footman on duty had to place a bottle of the best champagne by the side of Mr Field's bed and it was invariably empty by the morning. The head of the staff was the butler, of course, a Mr Devenport. He was a disciplinarian, but a very fair and good man and organized quite a large number of servants, including three footmen and several housemaids and kitchen-workers. We had a head cook and three junior cooks to prepare the meals.

Mrs Field allowed her dogs to sleep in her bedroom. She had as many as six at one time, usually whippets and Pekinese, and one even gave birth to a litter in the bedroom. Once, when she was ill and I had to show the doctor in to see her, he was rather disconcerted to see the bedclothes on either side of Mrs Field appear to rise of their own accord – and four dogs emerged! I had to excuse myself and go out of the room, or I would have collapsed laughing at the doctor's reaction.

Yes, she really adored her dogs and there was a special graveyard for them in the grounds. One night all the other dogs set upon one poor whippet in her bathroom and virtually tore it to pieces. Mrs Field summoned the vet immediately, who said it was in a hopeless condition and should be put down at once. But she refused to allow that, and told him it had to live. It took forty-seven stitches to put that whippet back together but it lived.

Mr and Mrs Field also had separate cars. She always used a Rolls-Royce, and he a Bentley. They changed them a lot. And they always travelled separately, even when they were going to the same function. There were three chauffeurs on the staff and quite a few vehicles, including some Mercedes in later years.

Madam – I always called her that – used to go shopping in her Rolls-Royce to Barnard Castle. But she never got out. The car would pull up outside various shops and staff would come out to take her order.

Mr and Mrs Field had expensive tastes. They only liked the best. The finest wines were always delivered and the food had to match. But the grandest occasions were always the Hunt Balls. I would help Mrs Field dress. She had some lovely gowns sent from London, and plenty of jewellery and pearls, and a diamond watch from Cartier. She did look beautiful as she made her entrance down the main staircase. And the gentlemen were so handsome, too, in their Hunt livery. Lots of titled guests were always invited and once, in my mother's time as cook, Princess Mary came to dinner. Their Christmas parties were very special, too, and they always gave one for their staff the night after the one they threw for their friends.

Although they had no children of their own they did adopt a baby girl from the convalescent home for children at Morris Grange. She was called Mabel, and came from Middlesbrough. They sent her to London for elocution lessons and she grew into a lovely young lady. Sadly, she died of a brain haemorrhage in 1950 when she was scarcely in her twenties.

There was more sadness in 1957 when Mr Field died at the age of seventy-seven. There was a big funeral and my husband, the head gardener, made a cross of fifty roses for Mrs Field to place on his coffin. She was stricken and missed him terribly, but she wouldn't show it in public. The only time we saw any of his family from America was at the memorial service. Just one came, and he was so like Mr Field he must have been his brother.

The parties went on at Lartington Hall but it wasn't the same place after the death of Mr Field. Olive went on with her public service, working for the Red Cross, going regularly to Morris Grange, and becoming the longest-serving Alderman in England. All this was recognized by an MBE.

The number of servants at Lartington Hall dwindled, although Dorothy Siswick stayed with Olive until the end. Her other

Mrs Field with Horace

In earnest conversation with Hannah (Courtesy of Yorkshire Television)

constant companion was a parrot named Horace. Olive steadfastly refused to move from the Hall, retreating gradually into the
east wing as the rest deteriorated. Birds nested in the
eighteenth-century ballroom but the chapel was carefully main-
tained and she also retained a butler and a chauffeur for the
Rolls-Royce.

Olive's spirit and capacity to command never diminished.
Apparently, she hugely enjoyed her part in the filming of *Too
Long a Winter* and liked the programme. When she saw Hannah
in the sequence where she played the tiny organ at Low Birk
Hatt, she tried to arrange for her to come to Lartington to try the
unique Aeolian pipe organ in the chapel. But, as Hannah recalls,
it was not to be.

No, regretfully Mrs Field died before it could be arranged. I
had only met her once before the film brought us together, but
I remember the occasion well. It was down the pasture near
Lartington on a day during the last war, when the weather
was very bad and I was going for the bus to Barnard Castle.
She was on foot going the other way, so I opened the gate for
her. 'It's awfully wild,' she said, 'but you are going the right
way' - she was proceeding east and going into the storm at the
time - and she thanked me for opening the gate.

Of course, everyone in the area knew Mrs Field - she even
owned two farms in Baldersdale, Foul Syke and Blackton. She
worked very hard for good causes and, during the war, in the
village and on the buses you often met servicemen in the light
blue uniform the wounded wore, who were recuperating at
Lartington Hall.

Hunting was a big part of her life, of course, and I have
mixed feelings about that subject. I'm well aware that foxes do
nasty things to lambs and poultry, and that sometimes there
are too many of them around. But maybe there are kinder
ways of keeping their numbers down.

Nobody thought anything about it during Mrs Field's
heyday. It was part of the way of life for the gentry, and not
the political issue it is today. A great social thing, too, and very
much part of the rural tradition. I have nothing against them

dressing up and riding around on horses but I don't like the thought of anything being hunted down, man or beast.

I have never seen a hunt in progress, although I recall vaguely as a child being taken to watch a Meet when I was visiting relatives in Piercebridge. I think it would have been the Zetland, and – who knows – Mrs Field may have been riding with them that day.

Nor, I must confess, have I ever seen a fox. Well, not a live one, anyway. Sam Fawcett used to keep a stuffed one in a glass case, which is the nearest I have ever been to one.

Less than six months after the transmission of *Too Long a Winter*, when her personality came through strongly enough to excite much public response, Olive Field was dead.

One of the sequences of the film featured Mrs Field being driven in her Rolls-Royce by her elderly chauffeur, Arthur Shields. On 20 June 1973, he was driving her, together with a friend, towards Morris Grange when their car collided head-on with a lorry. All three were killed.

This was a sudden and tragic end to a spectacular life. Olive was eighty-seven.

Nearly two decades after her death, they still talk about Olive Field in Teesdale. She has a permanent place in local folklore, and one story regularly told recalls the occasion when she and her retinue arrived at Darlington Station to catch the train to London. They were late – apparently, Mrs Field was invariably late – and as they approached the platform the train began to leave, whereupon Mrs Field set off in pursuit, bellowing 'Stop that bloody train!', in a voice richly laden with authority.

The message somehow got through to someone with the ability to obey her command – possibly the engine-driver, who may have thought it was an order direct from heaven – and the train ground to a halt. In front of a stunned and amazed assembly of railwaymen and passengers, Mrs Field boarded with a flourish and signalled her consent for the train to recommence its journey. Trains, taxis . . . they were all the same to Olive Field.

She was one of the last survivors of a lifestyle which is now extinct and despite the faint echoes of feudalism, its demise has made the world a less colourful place.

14

Ambition, Music, Politics...and the Future

H

annah Hauxwell is essentially a very private person. Her upbringing instilled in her certain strict ground rules, chief among which is modesty. Together these two factors have tended to cloak her personality, leaving an impression of excessive timidity. Those who know her well also know that this is inaccurate. She has strong opinions on several subjects, including politics, but not all for public consumption.

And she has nursed ambitions.

Hannah is obviously a natural musician, although the aforementioned modesty forbids her to agree with that assessment. But as a child she quickly learned to play both piano and organ with none of the pain and stress often endured by most youngsters, even those with natural skills. More than once she has been asked, without prior warning, to sit down there and then and play an instrument – usually for a film sequence – and she always complies without a flicker of nerves. She has often stated that, for her, music is one of life's most important elements.

It is a great pity that Fate placed her in a situation which allowed her no chance to properly exploit an undeniable talent.

If I could have asked for a gift, I suppose it would have been the ability to make a living as a musician. It must be marvellous to be an instrumentalist or a singer good enough to hold an audience in your spell, like Maria Callas or Yehudi Menuhin. But I would have had to be at the top, not just scraping along. And I would have wanted to be an instrumentalist, not a singer. Either the piano or the organ would have been my choice although, to play at concerts, I suppose the piano would have been the preference.

I have some sheet music which belonged to my mother, unless the mice and rats at Low Birk Hatt have chewed it to bits. But I can only play by ear these days. I could read music at one time but not now. Mother could play both by ear and by reading. But I have a theory that if you have two musicians, both trained and able to play anything that is put before them, but only one of them has the ability to play by ear as well, then he or she will be able to project more life, beauty and expression than the other. My late cousin, Norman, who was a very talented musician, shared the same opinion.

As far as my own taste in music is concerned I like everything from ragtime to opera, but prefer the classical composers such as Mozart, Beethoven, Strauss and Tchaikovsky. I'm old-fashioned when it comes to musicals, usually drawing the line after Sigmund Romberg. I'm not that keen on the modern composers, like Andrew Lloyd Webber. I wouldn't go out of my way to hear their music.

Not that I have had much opportunity to appreciate live music. I did once have the pleasure of going with Norman to hear Reginald Forte do a recital on the organ at Middleton in Teesdale Chapel, which is closed now. I do like a good organist, particularly when a traditional organ is used. I know they make some remarkable instruments now, electronic ones, I believe, which can produce all kinds of sounds, be it piano or clarinet or anything. And the people who can play them are very clever indeed. But that's not the kind of music I like.

I prefer the traditional organ, and I found out that Tony Benn also holds this view. We were appearing together at a literary lunch in Cleethorpes – he was promoting the latest edition of his diaries – and someone was playing the organ whilst we were eating. I heard him mention something about organs to another guest so I put my oar in and started such a nice conversation. It turned out that he shared my liking for the more conventional kind of organ.

Mr Benn is a thoroughly charming man, and I was pleased to pay tribute to him when I got up to speak. I like him for being a rebel, and we agree on several issues, although I am not sure I would go along with some of his proposals to abolish the monarchy and the House of Lords. But he has a good Christian upbringing and outlook.

Hannah with the 'rebel' she admires. A conversation with Tony Benn at a literary lunch. (Courtesy of Grimsby Evening Telegraph)

Now I know it's traditional for Daleswomen not to have an interest in politics, but our family was Liberal by and large. Uncle certainly was, and Great-Uncle John Tallentire was a great admirer of Lloyd George. I have used my vote in the General Election once or twice, but not recently.

Personally, I am against extremists of any political persuasion. I could point to quite a few leaders about whom I am not enthusiastic but I will refrain from naming them, and concentrate on those I like.

David Steel is one of them. Indeed, I recall one occasion when I heard him and Tony Benn separately on the radio and they were expressing essentially the same opinions about the same issues. I would have liked to have seen David Steel at

Number 10. I well remember him as one of the voices in the wilderness during the Falklands affair. Not many spoke out against sending the Taskforce – and I also admired him for taking over the Liberal Party in very difficult circumstances. I like several of his ideals, including, perhaps, the campaign for proportional representation. The present system does seem unfair.

Denis Healey is another politician I admire, and I tend to agree with the view that he is the best leader the Labour Party never had. He, too, has the courage to speak out, and so has Ted Heath, whether what they say is right or wrong or agrees with the party line. I like honesty but that is not possible if you are obliged to obey the party whip. I suppose a lot of people of different parties have similar ideals, good and decent Members of Parliament who all want the right things, such as the proper maintenance of the Health Service and provision of houses for the homeless. But they are not in a position to do anything about it unless they obey their conscience instead of the whip.

Power, or the prospect of power, is a very heady thing and some people cannot seem to cope with it. That's probably why there are so many different parties, why the Social Democratic Party and the Liberal Party split. I wonder if that is why we are stuck with the present regime – because there isn't a single, united opposition.

Personally, I would like to see a future government formed from all the parties as a coalition. Then they could all pool their energy and intelligence into solving all the problems we face.

As for my own personal future . . . well, I have my own Five Year Plan to sort out the confusion in which I live. But I think I may have to extend it – just like the politicians – because I haven't achieved anything in all the time I have been in my new home. I know there are a lot of boxes piled around the place. Some contain things which are valuable and useful and others, I have to admit, have stuff which I really ought to throw away. It won't be easy because of my hoarding instinct, but I shall really have to try. Yes, sorting out the house must be a major priority for the future, or else I will get into a real pickle again, like I did at Low Birk Hatt.

I do wish I could find more energy to get on with it. I'm afraid I suffer continually from tiredness, but the job will have to be done.

Looking ahead, I suppose travel would be nice, if only the opportunity arose and I had the courage to go with it. I have a wish to go to Paris. It would be lovely to walk along the Champs-Elysées and see the Arc de Triomphe, go into the Louvre to look at the Mona Lisa, and visit the Opera House. I have heard of a café near the Opera, where, if you sit long enough, they say you can see the whole world go by. That's the story they tell anyway. There are lots of other places I would like to visit – Vienna, for the music, would be high on my list – but I don't know how I would get there. By the shortest sea route probably, because the prospect of flying in an aeroplane rather daunts me.

But I have nothing at all to complain about. If I hadn't been 'discovered', as I suppose I must describe it, then I would have been on the same old path, up at Low Birk Hatt and miserable.

I know they say I am a celebrity, but I take it all with a pinch of salt. Fame is a very fickle mistress. I will enjoy it while it lasts.

I have a lot going for me. I have good friends, and if I can keep my faculties – if my eyesight behaves itself and my hearing stays good – then I shall be content.

Acknowledgements

Hannah Hauxwell and Barry Cockcroft extend their gratitude for unstinting assistance and support to John and Marie Thwaites, Mike Prosser, the Fawcett family, Margaret Nixon, Kelvin Walker, Lavinia Thwaites, Elsie Birdsall, Harold L. Beadle, Dr Philip Gates, Betty Pearson, Dorothy and Harry Siswick, Arthur Newlove, Derek Mayhew, Eric Stainthorpe, the new owners of Low Birk Hatt, Mary Hamilton, Betty Wall, Jim McTaggart of the *Teesdale Mercury*, Margaret Higginson, Sarah Wallace, Valerie Buckingham, Carol Hainstock, Barbara Bagnall, Brian Jeeves, Kathy Rooney, and Vivien Green.